MY MIDSUMMER MORNING

Books by Alastair Humphreys

Grand Adventures
Microadventures

Books by Laurie Lee
Cider with Rosie
As I Walked Out One Midsummer Morning
A Moment of War

MY
MIDSUMMER
MORNING

Rediscovering a Life of Adventure

ALASTAIR HUMPHREYS

WILLIAM
COLLINS

William Collins
An imprint of HarperCollins*Publishers*
1 London Bridge Street
London SE1 9GF

WilliamCollinsBooks.com

First published in Great Britain by William Collins in 2019

2020 2022 2021 2019
2 4 6 8 10 9 7 5 3 1

A catalogue record for this book is available from the British Library

ISBN 978-0-00-833182-5

Typeset in Bell MT Std by Palimpsest Book Production Ltd, Falkirk, Stirlingshire

Printed and bound in Great Britain by CPI Group (UK) Ltd, Croydon

MIX
Paper from
responsible sources
FSC™ C007454

This book is produced from independently certified FSC™ paper
to ensure responsible forest management.

For more information visit: www.harpercollins.co.uk/green

For Sarah

'Little darling, the smiles returning to the faces.'

'You asked for it. It's up to you now.'

'But I was in Spain, and to the new life beginning.'

Laurie Lee, *As I Walked Out One Midsummer Morning*

Contents

AND HERE I WAS at last. I had imagined this moment for years. My dream was finally happening. I had worked hard to make it this far, spurred on by the anticipation of how happy I would be. Yet now that it was beginning, I felt only afraid and lonely. I breathed deeply to calm myself. The air here smelled different from home – warm and dry. I looked beyond the pine trees and the red tiled roofs, over the blue bay, and on to the distant, forested hills. I wanted to flee and hide up in those hills. They looked so quiet and so safe. But I could not leave. At least, not yet. Before I escaped this town there was one task I must do, the burden that was scaring me. I needed to play my violin.

I was hungry. My pockets were empty. I had to busk to earn some money. But I had never busked in my life, never even played in public before. I was terrible at the violin. What on earth was I doing?

I could not bring myself to unpack my new instrument. Instead, I kept walking. I scrunched my eyes against the glare of the sun, crossing streets to cling to the shaded sides. My rucksack was cumbersome, heavier than I had imagined. I eyed a wishing well in a park. The water glittered with coins. I was both disappointed and relieved that the coins tossed in exchange for dreams were beyond my reach. It was a little soon to resort to stealing children's money and wishes. I prowled the streets, nervous, eyes to the ground, scanning for loose change. I was looking for money, but mostly I was searching for excuses. The well is always deep with those.

Eventually I made my way back to the town centre, to what I had already concluded – two or three times – was the best plaza for busking. There were no cars, but plenty of pedestrians. A church shaded one side from the sun. Let's get this over and done with, I told myself.

But my heart sank when I noticed that another busker had beaten me to it. A young man sat cross-legged in 'my' plaza, hunched over a recorder. This was not the time for an interloper! Usually, I would barely have noticed him: he was not a good musician and was playing very quietly. He wore a denim jacket and dark greasy hair fell over his face. He wasn't charismatic and did not appear to be very successful (nor even conspicuously, successfully destitute). But today, as I dawdled in the shadows across the plaza, I saw him in a different light. He was a musician! He knew how to play songs! Not only that, but he had been brave enough to snaffle the premium spot in town. His hat on the pavement already had money in it. I wished I could be like him. I wanted to ask how much he earned, to be in his presence, to seek his wisdom and his blessing. But I was too shy.

I slunk off and found a different plaza, sleepy and set back from the road. I dumped my rucksack by the fountain. The sun was high now, so I stooped to drink and splash my face. My back was sweaty. A waiter unrolled the sun shade outside his restaurant. '*Casa Gazpara,*' I read. '*Vinos, Comidas, Mariscos, Tapas.*' I remembered how hungry I was. I had only butterflies in my stomach. Some drunks swayed and slurred on the other side of the fountain. I couldn't even afford a dash of their Dutch courage.

I had not felt this apprehensive since the day a few years ago when I'd climbed aboard a small green rowing boat, picked up the oars and set off to try to row across the Atlantic Ocean. The prospect of playing a few tunes in a quiet plaza agitated me as much as colossal waves a thousand miles from land. But in place of storms and capsize, here I dreaded failure and shame. I was frightened of appearing a fool and worried what people would think about me. I knew this was pathetic behaviour for a man in his thirties, but the vulnerability was fascinating. What if I fall, asks the poem? Oh, but what if you fly?

I glanced around, then unzipped the violin case, furtively, as if it contained a gun. I was committed now, too far across the floor at the school disco to swerve my decision to ask the girl to dance. An apt comparison for I never dared do that either. I positioned the shoulder rest and tightened the bow. I had known that performing in public would be much harder than practising alone, which was why I had waited until today to try it. I had deliberately avoided getting accustomed to busking when the consequences did not matter. I chose to wait until it counted – until I was alone and penniless in a foreign country – because I wanted to experience the full shock of plunging in. I wanted to make this as hard as possible. I wanted that until I got it.

Pensioners watched the world go by from a bench near the fountain. They passed occasional comments to each other and pointed things out that caught their attention. One gentleman wore a Panama hat and yellow trainers; another was in a tweed jacket and dark glasses. Now they all turned in my direction, curious. I looked away, avoiding their gaze as I extended the legs of my new music stand. I tried to recall how buskers usually set everything up. I had never paid attention before. A gang of schoolchildren crossed the plaza, laughing and chatting. I pegged my music sheets onto the stand. A hush seemed to descend on the town and I stood lonely among the crowd. At this point a movie would cut to slow motion. I tuned the violin as best I could, fingers fumbling at the pegs. Don't die wondering, they say. Better to die on your feet than live on your knees, they say.

Die? Don't be ridiculous! It's only a bloody violin. *Lo siento, España*. I am so sorry, Spain. I lifted my face to the sun, smiled, took a deep breath, and began to play.

Imagine

SOMETIMES, WHEN I READ travel books, I say to myself, 'You could put this book down right now, step outside, and just go. The sunlit road calling you. Nowhere to be but there. The freedom all yours to choose.'

Imagine.
If I could go, would I?

A dusty white road winding through orange groves. Summer heat and the tang of citrus. Cicadas shrill the still silence. A silver ribbon of river threads the green valley below. A cluster of stone cottages and the dull clang of a church bell. The blue smudge of distant mountains. The day long and open and waiting for me.

As I hike, I cradle an imaginary violin, snug under my chin, fingers dancing on the strings. My right hand plays the pretend bow and I whistle the tune as I walk. One of the songs of my life, soaked deep into my marrow, personal and precious. I break from a whistled verse to yell the chorus.

Stamping the beat with my battered boots interrupts the rhythm of walking, but helps the exuberance bust out of my body. A song, a dance, a journey, all of my own.

The sun pounds and burns my back. But I relish it as a burnished medal for 20 miles earned each day beneath it. I have become lean but strong, stripped back. My pack contains the bare minimum, and that is enough. A blanket, bread, half a bottle of water. Strapped to the outside is my fiddle, the real one. It is fragile, smooth maple, and the magic key to this journey. Without it, I am ordinary – just another man tramping through Spain across the ages. But with this violin, I become a music maker and a dreamer of dreams. Tonight, beneath the stars in that village across the valley, I will bring music and laughter. My hat upturned upon the ground, dancers tossing coins as I play. They shine bright as they spin in the moonlight.

Wherever I walk, I sow happiness in my wake, and the world lies all before me. The weary satisfaction of physical effort beneath a summer sky. The focused simplicity of creating a living from the art you love. Carefree independence and the enticing spontaneity of the open road.

Just imagine.

If you could go, would you?

Life

I LOOKED UP. LET out a sigh. I was not in Spain, but somewhere near Slough, on a slow train bound for nowhere. I closed my book, a tale of sunshine, music and adventure. Monday morning trundled past, laden with drizzle and gloom. Flat-roofed pubs, warehouses, muddy park pitches. This was where I lived. This was my life.

Books carry me far away. I enjoy that, for I am cursed with *fernweh*, a yearning for distant places. Throughout my adult life I have either been wandering the world, preparing to, or wishing that I was. I grow excited every time I pack a bag and slip my passport into my pocket, but despondent when I arrive back home and put the passport away in a drawer. Returning inevitably disappoints, pricking my hope that going away might somehow have fixed my problems.

I first read *As I Walked Out One Midsummer Morning* when I was a student, dreaming of travel and getting ready to live. Laurie Lee had never left England before he docked in Spain in 1935. He hadn't given much thought to 'what would happen then, for already I saw myself there, brown as an apostle, walking the white dust roads through the orange groves'.

Laurie's hazy plan was to walk south from Vigo, exploring a new country and playing the violin to pay his way. He had no schedule or deadline. He slept under the stars, lived on bread and cheap wine, and flirted happily. Laurie's book is a paean to pure adventure, free from responsibility, made possible by the music from his violin. Reading it whisked me away to sunlit hills and villages, and I dreamed of one day following Laurie to Galicia. I wanted the same uncertainty, freedom and excitement in my own predictable, routine-dominated life.

But there was one fundamental problem. I could not play the violin, nor any other musical instrument. I had learned the piano for about a year when I was 10, until my mum yielded to the tedium of getting a reluctant, talentless boy to practise and allowed me to quit. I remember the music teacher at school – a bully later outed as a paedophile – mocking my timid and tuneless singing in front of a laughing class. I burned with shame and fought back tears. Forever after, I dreaded music lessons. Today, merely the thought of having to sing in public makes me prickle with nerves. I hate karaoke or dancing. My heart sinks whenever I hear the line, 'introduce yourself to the group and tell us a bit about yourself'.

Realistically, then, I could never busk through Spain. I had neither the skill nor the personality. Yet following Laurie's route with a wallet rather than a violin would be merely a walking holiday. That was missing the point. So, for 15 years, I shelved the idea. Instead, I looked elsewhere for adventure. I cycled round the world. I walked across southern India and the Empty Quarter desert. I crossed Iceland by packraft. I rowed the Atlantic, spent time in Greenland and on the frozen

Arctic Ocean near the North Pole. I was ridiculously fit. I hung out with intelligent, daredevil, ambitious misfits. Each expedition gave me ideas and skills for new journeys. They were miraculous days of joy and wonder. I even managed to turn these escapades into my career. I gave talks and wrote articles and books. I was the luckiest man in town.

But then, in life's musical chairs, the music stopped. And I realised I had been sitting in this threadbare seat for years now, staring out of commuter train windows. I called myself an Adventurer, but I was not living adventurously anymore. I was no longer proud of the story I was writing. The woman next to me, late for work and furious, tapped her displeasure in a series of to-and-fro text messages at my shoulder, clammy in her perfumed blouse. Tap-tap-tap. Pause. Beep-beep. Tap-tap-tap.

I shifted my focus to my reflection in the dirty, rain-spattered window. I didn't like what I saw. I was bored with myself. I had grown up and settled down. For most people this is the conventional, accepted route in life. I envy them. But it was not working for me.

I wanted uncertainty and doubt in my life, and the courage, energy and spirit to face them. I needed to move in order to breathe. I craved being on the road again, inhaling the heady air of places new with just one difficult but simple goal to chase. Instead, I was trundling round and round telling old tales to pay the bills. I had given up.

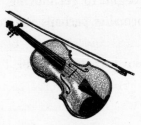

One Moment

I GLANCED DOWN AT the book in my lap, closed my eyes, and sighed. Then, without thinking, I pulled my phone from the pocket of my jeans, contorting myself on the cramped seat to do so. But instead of the artificial escape of social media, today I opened Google.

'Find a local violin teacher', I thumbed.

A website popped up, I found an email address, and before I had time to dwell on it, I began to type.

Fri, 20 Nov 2015, 11:56
TO: Becks Violin
FROM: Alastair Humphreys
SUBJECT: Can you teach me the violin really quickly?

Every journey, every change in direction, begins with one tiny deed, quick to revoke and easy to forget. An action so devoid of binding consequence that there is no reason not to take it. No reason except inertia and fear. The hardest part of every adventure is this one moment, small yet significant.

It is the decision to begin, to get moving, to push back the boundaries of your normality, perhaps even to turn your whole life around.

I hit 'Send' and went back to my book.

Laurie

LAURIE LEE AND I first met as teenagers, though he was 63 years older than me. Laurie lived in a lush valley in Gloucestershire where, emboldened by booze, he was busy getting his leg over with half the girls in the village. I was studying *Cider with Rosie* for English GCSE, avoiding eye contact with the teacher – all irascible nicotine and tweed – and willing the lunch bell to save me. Not for the final time, I envied Laurie.

Cider with Rosie is the story of Laurie's childhood. It is vivid with eccentric village characters and tales of his friends roaming the countryside. Laurie grew up in a chaotic but loving home with his mother and six siblings. One of his earliest memories was of a man in uniform knocking on the door to ask for a cup of tea. Laurie's mother had 'brought him in and given him a whole breakfast'. The soldier was a deserter from World War I, sleeping rough in the woods.

Laurie left school at 14 and went on to become a poet, screenwriter and author. He procrastinated prolifically in the pubs and clubs and literary parties of London. When he did write, he worked slowly with a soft pencil, editing and re-editing obsessively. Throughout his life, Laurie was plagued by self-doubt and often considered himself a failure, despite the unexpected, extraordinary success of *Cider with Rosie*, which sold more than six million copies. He described himself as 'a melancholic man who likes to be thought merry'.

The next time Laurie and I met, in our twenties, we were both looking for adventure. I was in my final year at university when I picked up an old copy of *As I Walked Out One Midsummer Morning*, the sequel to *Cider with Rosie*, in a charity shop at the end of my street.

'You'll enjoy that,' remarked Ziggy, the friend I was browsing with. 'It's about a guy wandering around Spain, half drunk with wine, and a bunch of dark-eyed beauties.'

Ziggy and I convened regularly in the greasy spoon café next door to nurse hangovers or refuel after frosty runs along the river. We spoke incessantly of travel and adventure ideas. Ziggy wanted to live in Africa. I wanted to hit the road. We were impatient for our course to end and the chance to charge across the start line into real life. Until then, I was burning off my energy with the university boxing club, muddy football matches and tomfoolery. It was fun, but what I really wanted was, once again, what Laurie Lee was doing.

Ziggy and I headed to the café with our small pile of books. I ordered mugs of tea while Ziggy found a table in the corner. He cleared a circle in the steamed-up window with his sleeve, then peered out. I took a slurp of tea and opened my new book. I have the same copy beside me today, faded and torn. It falls open to well-thumbed passages for I reread it almost every year.

Back then, I gorged on books about polar exploration and

mountaineering. These tales on the margins of possibility – the
best of the best doing the hardest of the hard – were exhilarating but unattainable to someone as callow as me. Laurie's
story was immediately different. It read like a poetic version
of my own life. The cover showed a young man walking towards
a red-roofed village under a clear blue sky. Bored with his
claustrophobic life, Laurie dreamed of seeing the world. He
didn't have much cash. His mum waved goodbye from the
garden gate. He felt more homesick than heroic. So far, so me.

I was disillusioned preparing for a career that did not excite
me as much as I thought life ought to. I had gone to university only because all my friends were going. It was a privileged
but naive decision, for it had literally not occurred to me that
it was possible to do anything else. I was training to be a
teacher, but dreaming of being an explorer. While my class-
mates sent their CVs out to schools, I researched joining the
Foreign Legion, the SAS, or MI6. I wanted mayhem, not
timetables. Today, it astonishes me how little I knew of life
back then that I saw only binary options: the Legion, or lesson
planning. Sensible and realistic, or thrilling but absurd.

'How does anything exciting happen in a blasted office?'
Laurie exclaimed after taking a job with Messrs Randall &
Payne, Chartered Accountants, when he left school. Laurie's
girlfriend urged, 'If it isn't impertinent to ask, why don't you
clear out of Stroud? You're simply wasting your time, and
you'll never be content there. Even if you don't find happiness
you'll at least be living.'

Soon after, Laurie wrote a brief resignation letter.

'Dear Mr Payne, I am not suited to office work and resign
from my job with your firm. Yours sincerely Laurie Lee.'

Direction

LAURIE LEFT HIS GIRLFRIEND and his home one midsummer morning and walked to London in search of fame and fortune. He had never seen a city before. He found work building 'three unbeautiful blocks of flats', pushing a wheelbarrow of cement through a tableau of Cockneys and con men whose priorities were petty theft, gambling and cheap cigarettes. A year later Laurie had 'little to show for it except calloused hands and one printed poem'. But he was saving money, biding his time and summoning his nerve. 'I never felt so beefily strong in my life,' he recalled. 'I remember standing one morning on the windy roof-top, and looking round at the racing sky, and suddenly realising that once the job was finished I could go anywhere I liked in the world. There was nothing to stop me, I would be penniless, free, and could just pack up and walk away.'

Laurie considered various foreign lands for his first adventure, 'names with vaguely operatic flavours'. But a pretty Argentinian girl had taught him a single sentence of Spanish, '*Deme un vaso de agua, por favor*'.

And so Laurie chose Spain.

* * *

Fifteen years ago, *As I Walked Out One Midsummer Morning* sang me a siren song in that Oxford café. I have been smitten by Spain ever since. I love the evening light laden with citrus blossom and the rook-like chatter of old women, dark-eyed and kinder than they let on. I fell, too, for Laurie's style of travel. He walked slowly and lived frugally (except after a windfall when he splurged extravagantly. Once he earned enough to buy 'a few litres of wine' and take a couple of girls up onto a roof terrace overlooking the city to share it). He camped on hilltops, bathed in rivers and enjoyed his encounters with the characters he met on the road.

Laurie shaped the way I came to approach my own travelling. Travel writers need not pretend to be infallible or invincible like the traditional stiff-upper-lip explorers. Journeys didn't have to be sensational or competitive. Adventure was not only for self-anointed 'Adventurers'. Laurie showed me a different outlook; that ordinary people could also see the world. I shouldn't feel like an imposter. All I needed to do was go. I didn't need experience or ability. Those I would earn along the way. This scrawny young poet gave me the guts and the permission to begin. Everything I hoped for in life was already out there, hiding in plain sight. I would only have myself to blame if I missed my chance at life. Enough then of the excuses!

I did not play the violin and so wouldn't be able to busk across Spain, but surely I could do something? I was giddy with the excitement of youthful possibility. My student days were drawing to a close and it was time to decide my direction.

I sat down at my desk, shoved aside football boots and coffee mugs, and rummaged for a pen. I stared for a while at a blank sheet of paper, then began to write.

Oxford,

December 2000,

Dear Mr. Walker,

Thank you for offering me a teaching position at your school. I would definitely enjoy working here on a permanent basis. However there is so much to see and do in the world. If I was to settle into teaching now I am sure that I would enjoy it, but there would always be something gnawing at me. Therefore I have decided that I am going to go ahead with my original plan to take two or three years cycling around the globe. Deep down I know that [teaching is] probably the sensible option. However, even deeper down I know that if I have the chance to do something now and do not take it, I may always regret it.

Yours Sincerely,

Alastair Humphreys

Adventure

Fri, 20 Nov 2015, 18:07
TO: Alastair Humphreys
FROM: Becks Violin
SUBJECT: Re: Can you teach me the violin really quickly?

Hi Alastair, Thanks for your email. Wow, what an exciting challenge! I'd love to help you out and am sure we could arm you with a few tunes (with some dedication!) for your adventure . . .
Becks

Becks

YOU CAN BE SURE that an adventure plan is good if the idea makes you simultaneously excited and scared, and you are unsure whether it is brilliant or stupid. One flippant email had set something in motion. A dream became a decision. I was going to follow Laurie into Spain, and do it properly: with a violin and without money.

The morning after I heard from Becks I walked into a musical instrument shop for the first time in my life. I was not in the mood for borrowing a violin to try or searching for bargains on eBay. I needed to move swiftly and decisively before my unrealistic fit of enthusiasm faded. I glanced at gleaming saxophones and trumpets, then walked past the pianos and drums towards a rack of stringed instruments.

'Good morning, sir. How can I help you?'

'I'd like to buy a violin, please.'

'Certainly, sir. We have a range of sizes and styles made from several different . . .'

I interrupted the shop assistant.

'Which one's the cheapest?'

He reached for a violin and presented it to me. It was the first time I had ever held one. I turned the instrument over in my hands a couple of times, feeling its weight and balance as though it was a cricket bat. It was lighter than I had imagined a violin would be. The assistant looked puzzled.

'Perfect. I'll take it.'

I had no idea what to do with my shiny new instrument. The thought of playing it for money was ludicrous. Nonetheless, I presumed it was a reasonable goal to learn a handful of songs before the summer. What should I choose? I allowed my mind to wander. 'Thunder Road', for sure. A Dylan song to appear bohemian, perhaps a jaunty flamenco tune or two. I'd learn them by rote and then turn up in Spain, ready to go. It would be tedious performing the same pieces over and over, but they should be enough to rouse a crowd and get them dancing in the streets. I pictured myself among spinning, smiling families and dark-eyed beautiful women or reclining in a mountain meadow with a feast spread before me – *empanadas* and *jamón serrano* and *manchego* cheese – and a bottle of *Albariño* wine chilling in the stream.

My first lesson changed everything.

I drove to my new teacher's house, chewing my nails, frowning at the satnav, slowing for speed bumps on the housing estate, peering through the windscreen wipers. I parked the car and dodged puddles on the pavement, the violin dangling awkwardly at my side. I felt daft pretending to be a musician and glanced around in case anyone was watching. My tendency to worry what people think was a significant obstacle ahead of me. I found Becks' house. It was an ordinary semi, the bins were full and the lawn needed mowing. I rang the bell.

When I had googled for violin teachers, it surprised me how many there were. Dozens of profile photos gazed out at me. How could I choose? There were plenty with glasses and neat hair: proper teachers, sensible and competent. Some were old and stern, others looked young, bright and earnest. Classical musicians, probably, teaching a bit on the side to get by. And then there was Becks.

Her photo showed a woman with waves of shoulder-length blonde hair standing ankle-deep in the ocean in a short black dress, clutching an electric violin. She had tattoos all down one arm and wore a skull ring. She glowered at the camera. Intrigued, I clicked her profile.

Background: world travels and touring with metal bands and rockers.
Musical influences: Iron Maiden, Slash, Prodigy, Tchaikovsky and Shostakovich.

I picked Becks.

She opened the door with a smile.

'G'day, Alastair. Come in!'

I took off my shoes and Becks closed the door behind me. I couldn't get out of this now. I followed her into the living room. A wizard's shield and sword hung on the wall. Large models of orcs and goblins stood to attention around the room. I tried not to stare. I suspected our lives were very different. But that suited me. I like people who walk an unusual path and have a different perspective. I wanted a teacher who would laugh at my incompetence, not frown. I needed someone who thought my plan was worth a try even if it was likely to fail. Someone who understood the restlessness.

'Sit down,' said Becks, offering the sofa. She had tattoos on her feet, and black nail polish.

I sat, grinned and set about explaining my idea. I told Becks about myself, about Laurie, those dusty white tracks, and how I needed to scare myself again, one last time.

'So, basically, like, erm,' I concluded, eloquently, 'I want to spend a month hiking through Spain next summer, without any money. I'm going to busk, like Laurie. But it is only going to work if you can teach me in time. We've got seven months. What do you reckon? Are you up for it?'

Becks laughed, an excellent Australian cackle.

And then we began.

I knew that a violin sounds famously terrible in the hands of a beginner. I had not realised the screech actually sends shivers down your spine.

I was going to fucking starve in Spain.

Music Lesson

BECKS GOT STARTED STRAIGHT away: pick up the violin, stick it under your chin and clamp it there. That's the ridiculous way you have to hold it, like a balloon in a party game. Don't worry; it's not a Stradivarius. Relax! You won't break it. Lightly balance the violin's neck with your left thumb, keeping your fingers free to position on the strings.

Where should you put your fingers, you ask, for you've noticed the violin has no frets to guide you like a guitar? Well, that's up to you: you must gauge the position, listen to the note and adjust your fingers accordingly. Hopefully, by the way, you tuned the strings: that's your job, too.

Now, grasp the end of the bow, loosely, with the fingertips of your right hand. You use this awkward horsehair bow (correctly tensioned and lubricated) to produce the note. Draw the bow across the strings, neither too gently nor too hard. Perfectly straight. Not too fast, not too slow. You'll get through these screeches, I promise. I'm afraid that's all we've got time for this lesson. See you next week . . .

*　　*　　*

Oh, Laurie, why did you inflict the violin upon me? In the hands of someone who has dedicated decades of effort there are few more beautiful sounds. Listen to Yehudi Menuhin playing Elgar's Violin Concerto or Bach's Double Violin Concerto. How can such divinity flow from the same instrument with which I just made those first awful screeches? My spine shivers even writing these words! I did not have decades to learn. I had seven months.

Progress

I HAVE SPENT MY adult life cajoling myself to work hard and make the most of my potential and my opportunities. I have coached myself to behave more boldly and be more optimistic than my natural disposition. Adventure entails taking on things that scare you, risking failure and pain in pursuit of fulfilment. One reason I gravitated towards physical challenges in remote environments was to make me uncomfortable and fill me with doubt. You put a little grit into the oyster if you want a pearl.

But the more expeditions I went on (what Wilfred Thesiger described as 'meaningless penances in the wilderness'), the more competent I became. My life of calculated risk began to lose the jolt of surprise that adventures were supposed to provide. This is the timeless addict's problem, the slippery slope towards bigger doses and greater risks. I could keep doing the same stuff, but higher, further, faster – pushing my limits, pushing my luck – or else something needed to change.

Centuries ago, the word 'adventure' meant 'to risk the loss of something', 'perilous undertakings' and 'a trial of one's chances'. An adventurer was 'one who plays at games of chance'. If I wanted to keep living adventurously, I had to veer from what I was good at and search again for uncertainty. Could something as gentle as learning a musical instrument count as adventure? I was beginning to think it might. The idea of busking terrified me. It was filled with risk, vulnerability, fear of failure and excitement. That was precisely what I wanted from adventure!

I quickly learned that the violin cannot be quickly learned. It is an idiotic instrument to use for enticing children to love music. It sounds hideous for a very long time. But Laurie crossed Spain with a violin, not something more beginner-friendly, so I was stuck with it.

I knuckled down to make the best of the time I had available, with a weekly lesson and an hour's practice every evening. Laurie also practised daily, though without the luxury I enjoy of a shed beyond earshot of the family. He sometimes overheard complaints from downstairs of, 'Oh Mum, does 'e 'ave to, 'e's been on all night'. I briefly suspected foul play from my own family when my violin got stolen. Someone broke into my shed one night, ripping the door from its hinges. But while I never saw my electronics again, I did stumble upon the violin a few days later, propped up carefully at the foot of a tree behind my house. I pictured the burglar's wife grimacing at his initial attempts, and him being sent back – in his mask and stripy jumper – to return the frightful instrument.

I was atrocious at the violin and needed to improve quickly if the plan was to become even vaguely viable. But I also discovered that repetitive rehearsal and incremental improvement had an allure of its own. Learning the violin demands deep concentration. As a compulsive multi-tasker, I found this forced focus calming. Late at night in my shed, my worries faded away for a while. I enjoyed the enforced humility of being a beginner and the mindful rhythm of committing to improvement.

I also glimpsed how enjoyable it must be to play music properly. Growing up, Laurie often played at dances in the village hall. He earned five shillings a night, plus lemonade and as many buns as he could scoff.

As adults, we rarely learn fresh skills or dare ourselves to change direction. We urge our children to be bold risk-takers, to show grit and open themselves to new experiences. We encourage them to try things like learning musical instruments. But us grown-ups? We hide behind the way we've always done things. We become so boring!

Adults are ashamed to be novices, and so we shy away from it. We draw comfort from being competent, even in narrow and unchanging niches. So we plateau and settle for the identity we have. We don't stretch ourselves because that risks failure and pain. In fact, it guarantees it, for the pain of being stretched is how we grow. You are vulnerable when you begin something new because you are exposing your weaknesses. I had not been so incompetent for decades. I was surprised to realise that it delighted me.

My lessons with Becks moved from her home to a local school. I waited my turn outside her classroom, listening to the accomplished scales and arpeggios of the pupil before me. I browsed the noticeboards and wished I even knew what an arpeggio was. My nerves began when his lesson ended and the corridor fell quiet. The classroom door opened. I could not believe how young the boy was. His school uniform was far too large for him, and I had to resist the urge to accidentally cuff him round the ear as we crossed paths.

However, I savoured both the intrinsic difficulty of the skill and my faltering but undeniable progress from note to scale to 'Baa Baa Black Sheep'. My favourite part of the lessons was when Becks took my violin and demonstrated a piece of music. I loved the magic that burst out of my very own violin, to hear what it was capable of. I was improving, but I was also running out of time. There was too much to learn. Every time I felt I was progressing, the next skill reduced me to a shrieking wreck again. Plucking the strings, playing a smooth note, moving from one string to the next, playing long notes, playing short notes, reading music, double stops, trills, vibrato . . . each week's homework was a dispiriting catastrophe!

My hopes for an eclectic playlist faded as Becks and I laboured through the tedious pages of *A New Tune A Day for Violin* (Book 1). There was not a jaunty flamenco in sight. My debut gig would be the Grade 1 Music Syllabus that thousands of kids across the land were also hacking their way through. Becks even invited me to take part in her pupils' end-of-term concert at the local primary school. The thought of being twice the height of the rest of the ensemble – knees round my chin on a tiny school chair – and the audience of proud parents was beyond even my levels of voluntary humiliation. I mumbled excuses, and Becks did not ask again.

Becks did a passable job of pretending she enjoyed my playing, fixing her face in to a pleasant expression of encouragement. Violin teachers must be a stoical, masochistic species. When you're going through hell, keep smiling. Only occasionally did she wince or let her mask slip. One lesson Becks set a metronome to accompany me. I sawed away at the strings, nodding to the beat. It was working! I was playing in time!

In my excitement, I fished for a compliment, 'Is this right?'

'Erm . . .'

Despite my dedication through winter and spring, as the days lengthened I could still play only a handful of tunes. Dylan was out of the question. In fact, busking was out of the question. Only Becks had ever listened to me play, and *I* had paid *her* for the privilege. There was no chance I could earn a living from busking.

As my planned departure day approached, I acknowledged, reluctantly, that trying to survive in Spain with no money was unrealistic. Everyone had been telling me this for months. The only sensible option was to postpone the trip for a year until I became competent, or at least travel with my own money and just do a bit of busking for a lark.

But fortunately in life, the only sensible option is not the only option.

I booked my ticket to Spain, and I began.

Into Spain

I SAT ON THE harbour wall, gritty and warm, with my face tilted to the sun. Sea salt and engine diesel in the air. Halyards clanking and gulls circling. Back in 1935, Laurie's ship docked in Vigo, a quiet corner of northwest Spain. Now I was here, too, at last. It was the first meeting of our paths since I had drunk in Laurie's old village pub, the Woolpack, while dreaming of this trip. I envied how vivid this arrival must have been for Laurie, setting eyes on abroad for the very first time. 'I landed in a town submerged by wet green sunlight and smelling of the waste of the sea. People lay sleeping in doorways, or sprawled on the ground, like bodies washed up by the tide.'

Here we go again, I thought: the start of an adventure. It had been far too long since the last one. I remembered the familiar belly-mix of nerves, melancholy and anticipation. After all the turmoil I had been through, I was jubilant that this was actually happening. I had thought these days were over. Laurie exclaimed, almost in disbelief, 'I was in Spain, and the new life beginning. I had a few shillings in my pocket and no return ticket; I had a knapsack, blanket, spare shirt, and a fiddle, and enough words to ask for a glass of water.' I had less money than Laurie, but more Spanish.

I picked up my rucksack and set off to explore Vigo. Graceful buildings flanked broad shopping streets, wrought-iron balconies on every storey. Meandering narrow alleys were hewn from rougher blocks of stone. A pail of water sloshed like mercury across the cobbles from a café opening for business, and I breathed the scent of geraniums. The waiter placed ashtrays on the wine barrels used as tables. Even after 20 years of travelling, I still cherish first mornings in a new place when every detail is fresh. Laurie described it as the 'most vivid time of my life, the most free, sunlit. I remember thinking, I can go where I wish, I'm so packed with time and freedom.'

It was mid-morning, but Spain still slept. The streets were so quiet that I said *'Buenos días'* to each person I passed. I climbed up to Vigo's old fortress and peered down from its mossy walls. Terracotta rooftops jumbled higgle-piggle down to the harbour. Wooded hills curved green embracing arms around the blue bay, sprinkled with islands. Earlier, boatloads of carefree beach-goers had departed for those islands, laden with picnic baskets. I had watched Africans trying to flog them sun hats, their wares spread on tarpaulins for ease of fleeing should the police appear. I sympathised with the urgency of their hustle, the immigrant's need to be enterprising. Like them, I had no money. I had been hard up before, but I'd never had nothing until today. Unlike the hat sellers, however, I was voluntarily penniless, so any comparison was absurd. I had a passport and permission to be here. At sunrise I had piled the last of my money into a small pyramid of coins on a park bench and walked away. I wished that I had bought a sun hat instead.

First Play

IT WAS TIME TO busk for the very first time. Throughout the morning I had hatched escape plans, justified delaying tactics and concocted excuses for compromise. But such self-destruction was not necessary. Not yet. For I had not failed. I merely had not begun. How our minds magnify that little step which separates where we are from where we wish to be! Leaping from a high rock into an enticing river; telling the boss you quit; speaking to the attractive stranger who keeps catching your eye: just one scary step gets us where we most want to be. But too often we flinch and build our own barriers instead.

The sun was high as I stooped to drink and splash my face in the fountain. The bleary drunks prodded each other and watched with bloodshot eyes. The fountain commemorated the *Reconquista* of 1809 when Vigo became the first town in Spain to expel Napoleon's army. Trees lined the square and on three sides there were stately nineteenth-century buildings. The fourth side lay open, leading towards a shopping street. The pensioners on the bench shuffled expectantly and the man in the Panama hat mopped his brow. I mumbled an apology for the disappointment that awaited them. I flicked through my music sheets to find the tune I was most comfortable with, a nostalgic old folk tune called 'Long, Long Ago'. I pegged it to the stand and took a deep breath. Then I began to play.

The ghoulish screech ripped the silence and my daydreams apart. Nails clawing down a blackboard. Shivers up the spine. I had hoped, somehow, that I might have become miraculously skilful since the last time I had practised. In fact, I was even worse than usual. My finger positions were all wrong and the bow trembled across the strings. Everyone turned in surprise. Screech, screech, screech! A sweat of shame and self-ridicule trickled down my face. Each note sounded jagged and raw. I lost my place in the music and had to begin again.

I threw my head back, screwed up my face and growled angrily. There was such a gulf between my ambition and my ability. The plan was doomed before it even began. I was an idiot. I had been too flippant, too idealistic. What a mess! I dearly wished I was not here.

It consoled me in my cowardice knowing that Laurie had felt much the same way before his initial attempt at busking. He was a proficient violinist, but he was young and beginning his first adventure. So perhaps we were about equal in our nerves. 'It was now or never. I must face it now, or pack up and go back home,' wrote Laurie. 'The first notes I played were loud and raw, like a hoarse declaration of protest . . . To my surprise, I was neither arrested nor told to shut up. Indeed, nobody took any notice at all.'

I stood in the middle of the Praza da Princesa playing 'Long, Long Ago' over and over. Beads of sweat ran down my flank and into my trousers. There was no crowd of fawning fans. No cascade of coins. Not even a round of applause. Just indifferent Spaniards accelerating past. I had known this would happen. But I had not known how it would feel.

The timid averted their gaze and lengthened their stride. The stoical reacted by not reacting. A businessman glanced up from his phone but didn't flatter me with a second look. A young woman in a leather jacket wrinkled her nose as though I stank. I was a visitor in her town behaving like a tedious fool.

I faced two options. Both were simple but neither was easy. I could stop playing, melt back into the streets and regain my blissful anonymity. It was so tempting. Or I could stick it out here in the plaza, daring myself to keep failing. If I quit now, the whole journey was over before I had walked a single step. I did not know how to catch rabbits, and I am more accomplished at foraging in supermarkets than forests. I had to earn money. I could not hide behind any excuses. I had no Plan B.

But what I did have was clarity. I had only one job to do. And I must do it with all my might. It was not easy, but it was simple. My legs shook. Half my head begged me to stop. But the rest of me, fists clenched, knuckles white, said no. Just finish this song. You can always ride one more mile, row one more minute, walk one more step, play one more song.

Hope

AN EMBARRASSED LAUGH BURST from my mouth
after yet another tune fizzled out. But this time a man on the
bench responded with a small smile. A smile! My busking had
earned something at last. This was progress. But it was only
a matter of time before people tired of me and the police
ushered me away, so I turned to my best song. 'Guantanamera'
was my jolliest piece and – being Cuban – vaguely close to
Spanish music.

'Guantanamera,' I explained, hesitantly, to the bench, after
stuttering through the closing notes.

'*Más o menos*, more or less,' said my ally, kindly. He was a
mild-looking gentleman of about 60, resting a pile of heavy
supermarket bags at his feet.

The men next to him continued to ignore me, stony-faced.
In their situation, I would have done the same. Make eye
contact with a crap foreign busker and he's certainly not going
to leave you in peace. Better to keep your head down and your
money in your pocket.

Back in England, Becks used to dish out musical advice above and beyond trying to coax me into playing some of the right notes in approximately the right order. One afternoon she described what to do 'once you've got a crowd gathered'. I raised an eyebrow at her sassy optimism.

'They will all be clapping along to this,' she proclaimed as I lumbered through a ponderous nursery rhyme. 'Spaniards are very rhythmical.'

I resisted asking whether she had ever been to Spain, and sighed. 'I honestly don't think a crowd is going to gather to listen to this.'

There was no solace in proving myself right.

My stomach rumbled but I had not earned a crust. It was time for what is always a good plan when you are vulnerable. Be humble, look people in the eye, acknowledge your faults, trust yourself, trust the world, smile, then try your best. I wiped my eyes on my shirt, tidied my music sheets and started again. Song after song, I failed to snare my first coin. Every tune was strewn with errors. But I was enthusiastic now, a less timid person than when I woke that morning. I had to persevere, be patient, keep hoping, and trust the people of Vigo.

After what felt like a lifetime sawing away, one elderly gentleman rose from the bench. He walked towards me, stooped and leaning on his stick. He looked smart in his dark glasses and tweed jacket, with neatly combed hair. I anticipated his words:

'*Señor*. Enough! Spare us. It is time to move on. *Por favor*. Give us back our peace, I beg you.'

But he did not say that. Instead, he put his hand into his pocket.

Surely not!

The old man pulled out a coin and handed it to me with a small smile. And I thought I was going to burst with exhilaration and amusement and relief. I had done it!

Nor was it just a copper coin. He gave me a whole euro! In the weeks of doubt before departure, my mantra to prevent me from wimping out of the trip had been, '*If* I can just get one euro, somehow, I can buy a bag of rice. With a bag of rice, I can walk for a week. Walk for a week and after that anything becomes possible. Just one euro. That's all I need. One euro. Somehow . . .'

That gentleman gave me much more than a euro. He gave more even than a bag of rice. For he gave me hope.

Encouragement

NOW: A COIN IN my case and hope in my heart! I had earned my first busking money. A euro! A bag of rice. A beginning. I held the coin up in the sunlight and kissed it. I was rich!

Laurie had a similar delighted epiphany that something as intangible as a mere song could be converted into cash. This alchemy revealed a world of possibility. 'I felt that wherever I went from here this was a trick I could always live by.'

Shorn of fear, I dived back into my repertoire, looping through my five little songs again and again, but this time playing with joy and confidence. It is probably no coincidence that more success followed. Two elderly ladies laughed at me, fumbled in their handbags, and gave 50 cents each. I had predicted that I would earn nothing in Vigo and that it might take days before I got my act together. I saw myself picking ears of wheat and pilfering crusts from café tables. But instead, I was rich on the very first day! And, like most wealthy people, I now wanted even more.

I sawed away, panning for gold, giddy and greedy with the

rushing release of nerves and the thrill of exhibitionism. And the money: so much money! I gazed in awe at the three gleaming coins in my violin case.

A lady strode through the plaza – jeans, blouse, smiling – aged about 50. She looked both prosperous and friendly: promising. She paused and peered into her handbag as though preparing to give me something. Then she changed her mind and walked on, flipping her hand at me. I presumed that she had noticed how bad I was. Oh well . . . nearly . . . At least someone had considered me.

Later, as I was packing to leave, the same woman returned, and this time she gave me a euro. She explained that earlier she had no change in her handbag. This was becoming decadent!

Laurie was also struck by gold fever, recalling, 'Those first days . . . were a kind of obsession; I was out in the streets from morning till night, moving from pitch to pitch in a gold-dust fever, playing till the tips of my fingers burned.'

A sturdy pensioner sat down to rest. He groaned as he lowered himself onto the bench, bracing his hands on his thighs. When he heard me playing, he did not smile. He watched with his jaw set and face expressionless. I grew nervous. After only a song or two he signalled me to stop, waving with his palm downwards in the Spanish fashion.

'Am I really so bad?' I wondered.

He beckoned me over and motioned for me to sit beside him on the bench.

I was rushing, the old man explained, playing too fast. I needed to allow space in the music.

'You know the expanding ripples when you throw a stone into a lake? That is music. The silences make a tune. The unique pauses are what make a life. My name is Antonio. Now, play me "Guantanamera" again.'

I returned to my violin. I left spaces. I played, as much as I was able, with passion. I really tried. When I finished the song, one of the drunks leaning on the fountain laughed and called out, '*más o menos*'. His pals showered me with the lightest ripple of applause. And Antonio dropped a coin into my violin case. It glittered with treasure like an overflowing pirate's chest. Four whole euros!

Antonio then launched into a rambling philosophical monologue that I only half grasped, explaining that my journey and my life was like the children's game *La Oca*. In *La Oca* you have to be willing to roll the dice and go for it. If you want to move forward, you must risk and accept whatever triumph or disaster comes your way. I was a free spirit, like the swan in *La Oca*, he said. I should feel proud of what I was attempting, and be as brave as I dared to be.

After a sleepless night and the day's exhausting emotions, Antonio's kind words brought a lump to my throat. It was just the rousing speech I needed to get me over the next hurdle. It was time to walk.

Preparation

I SCOOPED UP MY bounty and carted it to the supermarket. Up and down the air-conditioned aisles I went, fizzing with happiness, browsing carefully. I was not saddened by all I could *not* afford, only tantalised by how much I *could*.

How best to spend my money? I calculated fastidiously, focusing on calorie-to-price ratios rather than taste appeal. It was a good thing to consider every purchase. Too rarely at home do I ask, 'do I need this or merely want it?'

What if today had been beginner's luck though? The food those five shining coins granted me might have to last a long time. But I decided that I should never earn more than I needed when I busked, and nor should I hold any money in reserve. Boom or bust would keep me nicely on edge.

I made my choices – bread, rice, two carrots, an onion and tomato puree. I considered the smallest packet of salt, turning it over and over in my hands, but at 30 cents it felt too indulgent. I opted for an extra carrot instead, then carried my basket to the checkout, hoping I had done my sums correctly.

Only now, as I stuffed food into my rucksack, did I give

any real thought to the actual journey. Hundreds of miles of hiking lay ahead, alone, finding my way, sleeping outdoors, hoping for food. This uncertainty had not troubled my mind until now, proof that the concept of adventure ought to be broader than rugged men (or me) doing rugged stuff in rugged mountains. I had walked a long way before. I'd slept outdoors for months on end. I was comfortable with being uncomfortable. The traditional expedition aspects were what I knew well and had done many times.

I sat on the pavement, ripped off a chunk of bread, unfolded my map across my knees and studied it for the first time. It was the same brand I had used cycling round the world – Michelin – and the familiar cartography and design was reassuring. The shadings of higher ground, the red pin kilometre markings, the green scenic routes. But the specific unfamiliarity of this map also thrilled me. A new lie of the land to learn. All those fresh and unknown names. I tried the sounds on my tongue. Ponteareas, Vilasobroso, Celanova . . . so many unmade memories beckoning me towards them.

I planned to follow Laurie's route loosely, perhaps as far as Madrid. I had a month of freedom, and the capital lay roughly 500 miles away. I needed to get a sense of the distances I could cover out here, but that sounded about right. I had no schedule. I would just follow my nose and see where I ended up. I didn't mind. Laurie mentioned only a handful of place names in *As I Walked Out One Midsummer Morning*. These would guide me, but I wasn't concerned how I threaded the necklace. I was not aiming to replicate Laurie's walk, only to follow its spirit. I would find pearls of my own along the way. I brushed away crumbs, folded the map, flexed my knees to judge the weight of my pack and joined Laurie walking out into Spain.

First Walk

THE FIRST DAY WAS long, loud concrete drudgery. Before I even got out of Vigo I had to slog through the expensive, in-the-action central streets, the poorer rings of tower blocks, then the car showrooms, industrial parks, out-of-town shopping, and – eventually – the expensive, almost-in-the-country suburbs. Laurie did not suffer this misfortune back in the 1930s when the boundary between town and country was much clearer.

Pavements are hard and bruise your feet. I looked forward to the varied footfall of paths and fields. The day was hilly, hot, and my pack was bastard-heavy. It's difficult to find a place to pee in a city if you don't have a penny to spend in a café. City planners consider only cars. Their oily, noisy highways steal the best routes, choking, hooting, scaring me, and making plain the absurd slowness of walking in today's high-speed world. Pedestrians are neglected, or forbidden and forced onto circuitous routes. I walked with my eyes down, dodging dog shit, trudging through shredded tyres, broken glass and fast food plastic. Decades later, in the era of cars, Laurie reminisced about his Spanish experience. 'I was lucky, I know, to have been setting out at that time, in a landscape not yet bulldozed for speed.'

At last, though, Vigo was behind me, and I walked inland, away from the sea. A thousand rivers and streams had the opposite idea. They pushed past me, rushing towards the Atlantic. All of man's movements here had been channelled into this single valley, shaded with eucalyptus trees. There were no quiet parallel routes, nor could I head for open high ground and make my own way. If you leave Vigo to the east, this is the way you come. So I joined the procession. Cars, buses, lorries, and me: all going our own way. All, for now, going the same way. But I was the only one walking, and walking on a busy road stinks.

When I pedalled away from my front door to cycle around the world, aged 24, the scale of what I was taking on overwhelmed me. I was burdened by doubt as to whether I had chosen the right path in life. By going away, I discovered a deeper appreciation of everything I left behind. This heightened the significance of the unknown I had chosen in its place, and raised the stakes of my gamble.

Later, walking across India, I missed my new wife. I berated myself for trading comfy evenings on the sofa with Sarah for a lonely, ascetic hike. Three years later, however, by the time I was sweltering in the Empty Quarter, things had changed and I was just damn glad to be far from home. Laurie wrote of 'how much easier it was to leave than to stay behind and love'. But my disloyalty soured the relief of the escape.

Here, finally, on this July day in Galicia, I had the balance of emotions about right. This was precisely where I wanted to be right now. I was enjoying refreshing my Spanish, reading every billboard and shop sign I passed. I liked the novelty of my new hiking poles, and my shiny trainers felt good. I was neither too homesick nor too desperate to get away, nicely nervous rather than swamped by foreboding. I smiled thinking about Laurie's worries when he walked away from home. 'The first day alone – and now I was really alone at last – steadily declined in excitement and vigour . . . I found myself longing for some opposition or rescue, for the sound of hurrying footsteps coming after me and family voices calling me back. None came. I was free. I was affronted by freedom. The day's silence said, Go where you will. It's all yours. You asked for it. It's up to you now. You're on your own, and nobody's going to stop you . . .'

Off the highway by late afternoon, I followed an empty lane through sleepy old hamlets, home to more goats and chickens than people. The hot air smelled of dusty yellow grass. The landscape was more expansive than England's. It would be a long walk to each horizon. There were small mosaics of meadow whenever the land lay flat enough for vintage tractors to mow. Overhanging apple trees and unripe vines taunted my hungry belly as I eked out my bread. I pinched a grape, but spat it out – sour grapes for my theft.

Every village had a *fuente*, an old stone fountain. They were often shaped like a large gravestone built into a wall. A stream of water cascaded into a trough. I drank at each one, the water cold and pure, then dunked my head. I was pacing myself and taking care not to push too hard. Usually, I launch into expeditions hungover and sleepless from final preparations. I charge off with such enthusiasm that by evening I collapse exhausted, muscles screaming and sunstroke-dizzy.

A tetraplegic watched me from his garden up the hill. He was enjoying the sunshine in his wheelchair. I shouted *hola*, and waved. He could not wave back, but I hoped I provided a few seconds of distraction. When I feel caged by ordinary life, I told myself, I should think of that man, trapped inside his body, rather than feeling sorry for myself.

The rolling hills and heavy pack punished my unsuspecting legs as I climbed steadily towards a ridge of pines. The valley floor lay quiet and hazy far below. I waded through crisp bracken and ducked under the coconut fragrance of yellow gorse. I emerged in a village of steep alleys, stone cottages with closed doors and dogs going berserk at me.

A door cracked open at the noise, and an inquisitive old woman appeared, bent like a question mark. I raised a hand in greeting and called out that her village was beautiful.

'It is, if you like mountains, I suppose,' she grumbled.

'Do you like mountains?' I asked, hoping to elicit a more cheerful response.

'No.'

She slammed the door.

First Night

AS DUSK APPROACHED, I grew anxious. I was uncertain where to sleep. The amygdala, deep in the primitive brain, warned of the old dangers of the night.

'Play safe. Hide!' my instincts urged, tugging at me, keeping me safe, avoiding horrible imaginings, just as they had done before I busked. I knew I would have to camp every night, that hotels would never be an option on this journey. Right now I wanted to burrow deep into the woods and hide like a fugitive.

Then the voice of experience chimed in. It was low and quiet, but it reminded me that I have worried about the first night on every journey I have been on. Yet once I accept that I must do it and get on with it, I always love the simple act of finding my home for the night and making myself safe and comfortable. The memories of the past beckoned me down the road.

Given the opportunity, I prefer to head high and reach the top of the next hill before stopping for the evening. The views are better from a hilltop, the toil is behind you and you gift

yourself a gentle start to the next morning. Even when I am
tired, I reprimand myself if I put off the hard work until
tomorrow. Only in winter do I camp below a hill, when I will
appreciate the early climb to warm me after a cold night.

That first evening in Galicia I tossed down my bag on a
grassy hilltop in the lee of a eucalyptus tree. I flopped beside
it, peeling off my sweaty shirt and socks, and admired the long
views across the valley towards the sunset. Laurie might have
enjoyed the same view. There was not a building in sight,
though at times I heard distant sheep and dogs, a mile away
and 80 years ago. Breeze rustled the pale leaves above my head.
I sat cross-legged on my sleeping mat, lit a tiny fire ringed
with stones and perched a pan of rice on top. I hummed to
myself, enjoying the newness of being back in the old routine.

A plump, noisy bumblebee flew into his hole beside my bed.
He and me, our homes together tonight. A green woodpecker
rattled in the woods. The pan bubbled. I lifted it from the
flames to cool. The gloop smelled burned, but I salivated. I
ate half my rice as crickets chirped in the meadow, before
forcing myself to put down the pan and save the rest for
breakfast.

As dusk settled, I wriggled into my sleeping bag, sheltered
from the breeze. I was glad not to have a tent blocking the
view. The pink moon rose, gliding as it broached the horizon.
I love this part of the wanderer's day, watching the azure sky
thicken from cobalt to midnight blue and – eventually – darkness and sleep.

I reached for Laurie's book and turned on my head torch.
Its brightness reduced the world to only the text and pitch
blackness. Our journeys spanned the best part of a century.
The gulf of Hiroshima, the moon landings, air travel and the

internet separated our times. But the velvet contentment of well-earned rest beneath the stars bridged the gap and brought us together. Laurie was new to this outdoor life I loved. He took to it fondly. I read, 'Out in the open country it grew dark quickly, and then there was nothing to do but sleep. As the sun went down, I'd turn into a field and curl up like a roosting bird, then wake in the morning soaked with dew, before the first farmer or the sun was up, and take to the road to get warm, through a smell of damp herbs, with the bent dawn moon still shining.'

I have a tradition before falling asleep on long journeys: I choose my favourite bit of the day, and what I am looking forward to tomorrow. This habit stems from gruelling times when the magnitude of an expedition felt crippling, and the loneliness magnified it. It helps me to fall asleep feeling optimistic, for the day's last conscious thought to be positive before I surrender my brain to its unsupervised night of processing, filing and dreaming. There is always something good about each day, even if it is only the prospect of sleep. And tomorrow, too, will hold promise if I choose to see it, whether in a cup of tea, anticipating rest at day's end, or the glory of reaching the furthest shores of a continent.

I ached, yawned and smiled: a sweet cocktail for sleep. I had earned this rest. As I do every night, I whispered goodnight to my family, using my wife and children's nicknames. It brought a brief knot of sadness to my belly. The moon cast shadows over the field. It was peaceful on the fringes of the wood. Nobody knew I was there. Today, I had stood up in public, played the violin and passed my test. And I had walked. I had done everything the day asked of me. My journey had begun.

Marriage

BY THE TIME I finished cycling the world I was skinny, skint and spent from four years of singular focus, ascetic living and tens of thousands of lonely miles. Soft beds hurt my back, social gatherings made me anxious, supermarket aisles looked impossibly decadent. Reflecting on this, it is not surprising that such an experience eroded and hardened me in ways that would take years to resolve, some of them only with writing this book. Your first adventure moulds you; everything after fits into the impression it made. But I was unaware of all this. I only knew that I was proud to have achieved something exceptional for the first time, relieved that it was over and happy to be back with Sarah.

I had loved Sarah for years before pedalling off in tears. I was sad to go but too restless to remain, convinced that there must be more in the world than I could find at home. Sarah didn't want to come with me: a decent job and a hectic social life sounded better than banana sandwiches, a tiny tent and endless bloody cycling. After four years apart, I threw my frayed cycling clothes in the bin, put my penknife into the cutlery drawer and moved in with Sarah.

We were very different, but our worlds sat together comfortably. Sarah wore a suit, went out to work for a big firm of accountants and then came home to relax in her pyjamas with DIY and soppy TV shows that made her cry. Uncertain what my future held, I wrote my first book, sitting at home all day in my underpants. I gave talks at schools (fully dressed) and trained for a marathon. I needed Sarah's cheerful confidence and competence, her poised assurance that life was mapped out and under control. I'm not sure what was in it for her. Sarah is not interested in the things I love: expeditions or books or exercise. Corporate tax is not my strong point. So we helped each other keep things in perspective. Opposites fit snugly in a jigsaw.

I was halfway through a 20-mile run on a cold autumn morning when I decided to ask Sarah to marry me, slipping and sliding along a muddy footpath by the Thames. Rain lashed my face. I love running in weather like this. As I ran, I imagined two routes in life. I was sorry I could not travel both. One was the open road, with all the world to explore, and the joys and struggles and lessons that would unfold. It was selfish, feral and solitary, but tempting as ever. The alternative was unknown: marriage, children, a different search for fulfilment. A family, and all our joys and struggles and lessons together. Without these connections, I feared I would become a rootless drifter.

A cracking story is not a life. Knowing how way leads on to way, I made my choice. I was still eager to explore the world, to keep pushing myself hard and to make the most of life. But I looked forward now to sharing that with Sarah.

I jumped into the river to confirm that I was thinking straight and hadn't gone mad, then ran back home to ask Sarah if she would like us to spend the rest of our lives together.

'I take thee, Sarah, to be my wedded wife . . . from this day forward, for better or for worse.'

'With this ring, I thee wed.'

We left our wedding reception riding a red tandem – tricky for a bride in a long white dress – with fireworks bursting overhead. As our honeymoon plane curved its great circular route over the Arctic, Sarah slept, her head against my shoulder. Her blonde curls covered her face, and I gazed out of the window at the endless expanse of ice below.

My wife and I clinked bottles and sipped cold Big Wave beer in the Hawaiian sunshine. The sound of the ocean carried to us on the warm breeze. But that beguiling Arctic ice lingered in my mind. To my surprise, I sensed that my tide of post-cycling exhaustion had finally receded. Were those years of yearning for stillness and community being pushed aside again by the clamour of restlessness and ambition? Polar literature had always entranced me, and I pondered the enormity of Antarctica. Endeavour, endurance, discovery: could I hack it there? The prospect was both terrifying and thrilling.

I despised being a one-trick pony, that guy who had once done something interesting and never stops talking about it. I have had a fortunate life and the only challenges I've faced are those that I have set myself. My ego, and my desire to be acknowledged as a serious adventurer, demanded a new trip.

I had become beguiled by the macho lure that bigger is better, that expeditions were a way of sorting the strong from the weak. (Laurie wasn't immune to this either. Long after walking across Spain, he admitted that part of his motivation had been to show off to girlfriends.) I was, to borrow from Robert Macfarlane writing about mountaineers, 'half in love with myself, and half in love with oblivion'.

Feeling a little guilty, I put down my beer bottle and sloped away from the poolside to email a friend.

Hi Ben,

Having a wonderful time in Hawaii – been out whale-watching and running this morning.

But I can't stop thinking about my future expeditions. So I decided to write and ask in all seriousness if I can join your South Pole expedition? I am writing because I will regret it if I do not, but also because you know me well enough to be able to say 'No!' without embarrassment or worry . . . !

Look forward to chatting in the New Year when I get home. Hope you have a warm, sunny Christmas, like me,

Al

There were already three of us competing in this marriage: Sarah, me and adventure.

Dawn

I STIRRED IN THE silent hues of dawn, shivering. Too cold to sleep, too cold to get up. I lay uncomfortably for a while before conceding that I would not fall back to sleep and the morning might as well begin. The hills of Galicia were colder than I had expected for the summertime. I stood, stretched and dressed. My sleeping bag was dew-damp as I stuffed it into the rucksack. Yawn, blink, pack, leave. Into the distinctive moist-earth smell of the early hours, the air raw in my nostrils. It was still dark, but there was enough moonlight to walk without a torch. I padded through villages, the only soul astir. Valeixe, Vilar, Crecente . . . It was hard to keep heading east on roads that hairpinned and looped as they hugged the contours of the hilly landscape. This early, I was content to walk along country lanes to speed my progress. When the world woke and cars returned, I would return to the fields and footpaths.

The road was a single lane of potholed tarmac, crumbling at the edges, among smallholdings of corn and grapevines. A white dog pricked its ears as I filled my bottles at a village fountain, but it offered only a couple of sleepy barks of protest. The water glinted as it splashed, and sounded loud in the stillness. A solitary streetlight darkened the dawn sky around it. Barns and dry-stone walls were built from blocks of lichen-mottled stone. I ran my fingers along their gritty surface and sprouting clumps of soft moss. A rose bush spilled over a garden wall, and even this early the scent was strong. As the moon set in the purpling west, colour crept back into the world. Morning had returned.

Then the rising dust as the dew dried, the coming of heat and the yeasty presence of farm animals. A pair of blackbirds hurtled across the lane at ankle height, pouring torrents of noise at each other. In the passing blur I could not tell if they were courting or scrapping. A common confusion. My shirt, damp from yesterday's sweat, steamed with my body heat in the early light. A church bell and the distant jangle of sheep bells amplified the quiet. It was many hours before I spoke to anyone. I reached into my pocket for some bread. It was so stale that I had to use my molars to tear off lumps. I didn't mind, for it made the enjoyable act of eating last longer. I set a brisk pace as there was a village on my map that I hoped to reach in time for a lunchtime busk.

The first time Laurie played his violin in Spain he was frazzled from the sun, and a glass of wine had gone to his head. He 'tore drunkenly into an Irish reel. They listened, open-mouthed, unable to make head or tail of it.' Then he tried a fandango and 'comprehension jerked them to life'. An old man danced 'as if his life was at stake' and afterwards 'retired gasping to the safety of the walls'. Laurie went on to play in markets, inns, cafés and the occasional brothel along his journey. His instrument became 'a passport of friendship'. I hoped that might hold true for me. But I was certainly never going to be allowed to perform in a café, never mind anywhere more exotic.

My prompt start got me to the village in good time. The school playground was lively and noisy and I hoped the same would be true of the plaza. My timing was good: the café was busy and customers were walking in and out of the bakery, the bank and the small grocery. I rested on a bench for a few minutes, drank some water and ate a carrot. Then it was time to busk.

Nobody ever stopped and listened to me play. This was partly because I was hopeless and my music was not pleasant to listen to. But it was also because you become trapped if you stop. It grows awkward to leave. So when a grandmother paused in front of me with her two young grandchildren, mid-song, my hopes rose. They faced me in a row, holding hands. She nodded along as I worked through the notes, my brow furrowed and tongue poking out of the corner of my mouth. Sunlight sparkled on grandmother's glasses. A dead cert, I thought! Time to play well and be charming. When I finished the song I smiled, looked down at the children, and asked whether I was good or bad.

'*Bueno*,' mumbled the boy, staring at his feet. He did not sound convinced.

The *abuela* laughed, tousled his hair, then turned the boys away. I could only watch as they walked off down the street, laughing. Damn! I took a drink from my bottle, turned the page on my music stand and began again.

The Pram in the Hall

I HAVE BEEN A father for nine years. It has been the hardest journey of my life.

On my wedding day I felt such a fullness of emotion. Truly, this was what it was like to love, to commit, to share. But even that joy was dwarfed by the birth of my children. Tom was born under a half moon, on a cold and windy night in the autumn. Lucy arrived a couple of years later on a sunny Sunday afternoon. Holding a newborn in my hands over-whelmed me with a fathomless ferocity of love. The old conundrum of whether you would lay down your life to save another does not apply to your offspring. No question: I treasure my children's lives far above my own.

But here is where my difficulties began. For I still cherished my own life, separate from the family. And though I would leap heroically in front of a train for my children, I struggled to make the less glamorous daily sacrifices that the roundabout of parenting demanded – the endless cycle of feeding, Peppa Pig and nursery rhymes playing on loop in the car. I wanted to hold onto my old self, but it felt impossible. *My* life became

consumed by *our* life. I found the comedown to the routine of
babies and suburbia excruciating after chasing a deliberately
unconventional, varied, selfish existence. The trouble with
filling so many years with adventure was that 'out there' came
to feel more like 'out here'. Life back home was unsatisfactory
and bland by comparison.

I wanted to be around my children, to be a big part of their
growing up, to share the work equally. I loved the laughter,
story times, play fights and first steps. I was absurdly, tribally
proud of everything they did. I wanted it all, but I couldn't
handle how claustrophobic life became.

'It's only a phase,' I heard. 'Give it five, ten, twenty years
and then we'll get our lives back.'

This was offered by parents as casual consolation to each
other in rainy playgrounds, one hand pushing the swing, the
other thumbing through their mobile phone. But 'five, ten,
twenty years' rang alarm bells at me: this was a vast proportion
of the life I had left. It panicked me rather than reassured me.

Many people – the pragmatic, glass-half-full, my-glass-is-big-
enough type – cope with this. Sarah was one of those optimists,
nattering with other mums about the daily triumphs and disasters of parenthood. The small victories outweighed the drudgery,
tilting the scales towards a life adequately well lived. I envied
their contentment.

It was undoubtedly enriching to care for small children
without expecting personal gain. Their excitement as you
offer a bowl of mushed banana, the astonishing speed of
learning and tireless curiosity. But I also felt angry and discon-
tented. I had spent too long marching to my own drum to
enjoy spending years drowning in plastic toys and row, row,
rowing my boat down the bloody stream.

*   *   *

As I folded myself into this new life, I turned into a person I no longer liked. I became mean, impatient and sullen. Unkind to those I loved most, I was present but emotionally distant. Over the years, it ate away at my soul, leaving a void filled with bitterness and despair. I worried whether I would ever rid myself of it.

A group of cyclists whizzed past me as I was out pushing the pram. They were enjoying being together and riding hard. I sighed and glowered.

'I once cycled around the world!' I screamed in my head.

I made myself numb, traipsing listlessly through the routine, training myself not to feel, not to think, just concentrating on making it through each day. I stared at the microwave clock as it counted down the minutes needed to sterilise a milk bottle, and dreamed about Antarctica. I drove aimless laps of the neighbourhood until the wailing in the back seat softened to sleep. I seized upon errands in order to escape, busting out on urgent missions to the recycling bank or the local tip – particularly when I hoped there might be a long queue. I dreaded weekends and holidays. I willed the claustrophobic hours to crawl by. I was appalled as the years galloped on, my allotted share spilling into the dust. Time slips away and leaves you with – what?

I had been so enthusiastic and idealistic about life. But, to my surprise, I lost that with the arrival of children, replaced by a heavy feeling of worthlessness. The days pressed down upon me, and I moved through the murk in a drained, listless daze. I mourned my loss of freedom, confidence and time – the three things Laurie considered he had won with the success of *Cider with Rosie*.

There were many times of acceptance and joy amidst it all,

of course. But there were too many occasions when I came damn close to walking out, slamming the door and never looking back. Only a sense of duty stopped me. Kept me rocking cradles, changing nappies, catatonic. I had travelled the world. I get paid for having adventures. I married the woman I love, and together we had two happy children whom I adored. I was a lucky man. So why was I so sad?

Over many years I had managed to build a viable career as an 'Adventurer'. It had been hard work, but I loved every bit of it. I was a perfectionist, unable to relax, never satisfied, always competing and striving for more. Expeditions made me confident and goal-oriented. They also, perhaps, gave me unrealistic expectations. I refused to accept that life should be anything other than a daring adventure. But I was profoundly ashamed of how selfish this made me feel. I was raising my own children – seeing the epic adventure of their lives unfold – and yet I wanted *more*? I detested grasping time, aware that I was short-changing both my life and my children.

Sarah's career tied her to a City office so we couldn't live in a van in the wilderness. Instead, like most families with two working parents, we had too many plates to juggle. Life fragmented and turned stressful as we cancelled plans, texted terse apologies for delayed trains and rushed around in an exhausted blur. Despite all this, Sarah had much that she dreamed of – a career, two kids, her family nearby, a vegetable patch and weekends at home. But I made it miserable for her with my frustration, souring the joy of motherhood, and offering no sympathy for her hard work and sacrifices. I wanted somebody to blame, and that was invariably Sarah.

I was trying to force myself into a box that most people want to be in. All my friends (except the adventure crowd) were in that box. Everybody where we lived was in it. But I couldn't do it: commitment clashed with freedom. Ambition glowered at the pram in the hall.

Swifts

A HUNDRED YEARS OR more seemed to hang in every siesta. Streets and plazas deserted, the clocks and the world all stopped. A momentary breeze tumbled an empty cigarette packet along the pavement, then all was still again. Spain has a drugged afternoon listlessness, minutes and hours creeping by, oceans of glare beyond islands of shade. As the sun turned, shadows crept across the ground, eating up my hideout and the remains of my rest. Clouds formed, twisting into fantastical shapes, then faded.

I followed the swirl of swifts with my eyes, never tiring of them, exhilarated by their audible 'whoosh' as they hurtled over where I lay in the lee of a wall or tree. They were constant companions through the summer, slicing like knives through the sky. I enjoy seeing something familiar in an unfamiliar place. It roots the thing and the place in my mind. I remember a Champions League final in Kazakhstan, the death of a royal in the Nubian Desert, a Bactrian camel as I ran round Regent's Park. Now it would be the screeches of swifts and violins that I connect.

At home I anticipate the swifts' return each year, keeping an eye on the square of sky above my garden, framed by the branches of an enormous pin oak. They herald the end of winter gloom and the approach of summer. Swifts are restless wanderers, always in motion, surging at the horizon, battering against their constraints. When they are here, they are thinking about there. And when they are gone, half the world away, they are readying themselves to return. Too much energy to remain, but condemned to feel the same way once they escape to there.

The long afternoons in drowsy towns merged into one another. Heavy eyelids, only flies and swifts on the move. The faint sound of a radio. The smell of someone frying their lunch. I was a stray dog, unminded and free, with the streets all to myself.

Kleos

ADVENTURE WAS INCOMPATIBLE WITH settling down to bring up small children for many reasons, even without considering the type of personality who seeks adventure in the first place – driven, solitary, reluctant to settle. Cycling around the world had showed me it was possible for an ordinary person to live extraordinarily. I learned that I was capable of doing what I dreamed of, not just dreaming about it. That revelation removed the cloak of excuses I used to wrap myself in. It opened Pandora's Box, both the greatest privilege and curse of my life. Without the excuses, all that remained was a vulnerable soul who had to hold himself accountable for his fleeting hours and days and singular life.

I believed for years that adventures had to involve fine margins and grave consequences. There needed to be a tacit willingness to court disaster. Not many job descriptions include that. But my attitude to risk changed with fatherhood. I still craved difficulty, but now I abhorred danger. Rowing across the Atlantic, I was filled with overwhelming guilt knowing that I had left behind my toddler, baby girl and wife.

It would be a magnificent jape if all went well, an excellent story for the grandkids; but what a stupid, selfish fuck-up driven by vanity should it widow Sarah and leave my children fatherless.

You cannot go alone into the wilderness for months and also be a stay-at-home dad. You cannot teeter across a crevasse field without feeling somewhat reckless. And when I did manage to get away – to make a short film, for example – I knew people frowned on it as 'going on holiday' rather than 'going to work'. This generated resentment on both sides. Everybody except me seemed to have a clear idea of how I should lead my life. My life, my work, my hobby: it was all the same thing. It was me. And now it was gone. Ben and I were still training for the South Pole, but we had not yet secured the funding we needed. Everything I thought of as 'me' collapsed. I could not compartmentalise things in the way most new parents do, swapping stuff around, cutting down on hobbies, or pausing bits for a decade. If I was not me anymore, then who was I?

I had become an Adventurer who no longer went on adventures.

What I should have done was exchange all that I used to be for my new role as a parent. To walk into the phone box as *Adventure Al* and emerge proudly as the heroic new father, a modern man in three parts: father, husband, individual. Instead, I believed I had become nothing at all. Some call me brave for the journeys I have been on, but I did not have the real courage demanded for submission, to reconcile my life, to give it new purpose and value, and to embrace becoming a dad.

* * *

Stuck at home, I turned to the gym as an outlet for my resentments, picking up heavy stuff, throwing it back down. Fifty kilograms. One hundred. Day by day, perseverance pays off: 150, 160, 165 . . . But gyms are boring when you have nothing to train for. So every few months I would tire of deadlifts and turn instead to beer, slurping cans on the sofa – four, five, six – watching my life slide out of view, while Sarah WhatsApped her friends in the bath then went to sleep. I seem to do everything to extremes, whether that is expeditions, exercise, or boozing.

As the world raced on without me, I grasped at different ways to cope. I signed up for an Ironman triathlon. Training opportunities would inevitably be constrained. That was fine: I was willing to accept just scraping through the race rather than doing my best. But one Saturday, sprinting in a fury on a quick training ride snatched between morning childcare and the inevitable afternoon kiddy party, I cracked. I jumped off my bike at the top of a hill, gasping, then flung it over a hedge and howled at the sky before falling to the verge.

'FUUUUUUUUUUUUUUUUCK!'

Eventually, when all the tears had dried up, I glanced around to see whether anyone other than the cows had seen my antics. Then, feeling slightly silly, I squeezed through the hedge in my clumpy cycling shoes and unflattering shorts, extracted the bike from the field and straightened the handlebars. I cycled slowly back down the hill, and home to cancel my race entry. I was learning that lowering my aspirations was the best way to reduce disappointment and conflict. If I did not have plans or dreams, they could not wither. Only by giving up on my life did it seem possible to live.

* * *

I was nagged by insecurity that people thought less of me now that my adventures had dried up. The ancient Greeks called this *kleos*. *Kleos* is not only your feats, but also the glory of being acknowledged for them. Achilles faced the choice between the dazzling *kleos* of being a warrior slain in his prime, or the anonymity of a peaceful life at home on the farm with his wife and son. I always used to think that he made the wrong choice. Yet now I yearned for the same destiny – for the bubble reputation – to burn, burn, burn across the stars.

I still made my income from speaking, getting paid to give presentations about living adventurously. I was talking a good life but not living one. I flew to America to speak at a conference, to walk on stage in the spotlight before a thousand people eager to hear my stories. They treated me to business class, but I felt a fraud. I got smashed over the Atlantic – fancy red wine on tap – and landed in a worse state than everyone back in economy. I hated dredging up my old tales, telling audiences about my glory days, what I used to do, who I used to be. The crowd cheered. I cried all the way there and back.

At every talk I gave, every social event I went to, in every interview, I was asked the same question. It continues to this day. I dread its inevitability.

'What adventure are you planning next?'

And I wanted to scream, because 'nothing' was not an acceptable answer – for them or for me.

Reverence

I WAS TIRED, HUNGRY and anxious. I had not managed to busk for several days. I surveyed dozens of café chairs and white umbrellas arranged around the plaza. Prime busking real estate. But the square was virtually empty when I arrived in the afternoon, hot and aching like Laurie. 'After the long day's walk my back was sheeted with sweat and my bag was like a load of stones. I slipped it to the ground and sucked in the hot still air.' A couple of lads idly thumped a football around, using the town hall doors as a goal. The ornate monastery of San Salvador de Celanova loomed over the town. An imposing building of huge stone blocks and gargoyles, it was – predictably – closed. I cupped my hands round my eyes and peered through a sturdy wooden grille on the door. Inside it was dark, but sunshine spilled from the central dome and all the gold on the altar gleamed.

Despite my eagerness to busk, there was nothing to do but wait. I filled my bottles from a fountain and looked for somewhere to rest until people returned to the streets. I flopped in a side plaza, leaning against the limestone walls of a parish church. It was a relief to take the weight and shoes off my feet. In the distance I could see the forested hills I would cross tomorrow. Sparrows chirped overhead in a grid of plane trees. The trunks were broad as temple columns and the branches had been pollarded so that the canopies wove together to create a roof of shade. It was a charming place.

A dozen children appeared on bicycles. They separated into two gangs. One bench for the young kids fooling around, their banter so quick that I couldn't keep up. The second bench for the teenagers – two girls, two boys, too cool – bowed in silent worship to their phones.

Meanwhile, choral music played from speakers inside the church. The plainsong chants lured me in. The door was open, so I entered the cool darkness. Dust motes floated in beams of sunlight among the incense and music. As my eyes adjusted, I ambled down the nave, holding my sun hat in awkward reverence. I sat in a wooden pew and closed my eyes. Time flowed by, the abundant hours of the afternoon. The music continued, intricate and layered. Deep gratitude swelled inside me. The swifts still swooped outside, but their cries were faint now.

When evening came, I went out into the streets to busk and earned enough to buy bread and tomatoes. Then I walked out of town to sleep in a field.

Polar

MY VOICE CHOKED WHEN I began to speak. The south London pub was quiet. There were a couple of lunchtime drinkers over at the bar and a low murmur of conversation. I looked away from Ben and concentrated on ripping my beer mat into pieces. The fruit machine flashed and jingled.

With hindsight, trying to combine marriage, children and adventure was asking for trouble. Sarah generally endured my whims, but the pressure built and every so often a spark ignited a ferocious argument. They invariably ended unresolved and in tears, with Sarah going to bed and me drinking beer in the garden. The spectre of the South Pole expedition loomed over us.

What should I choose? A four-month adventure to the ends of the earth, leaving behind two young children and my frazzled wife? That choice seemed destined to lead to divorce. It was unfair on my family to go away for so long on a dangerous expedition, however significant the goal was to me. Or would I stay at home, turn away from one way of life and try to become somebody different? To be a dad and a husband, not a hobo. I could no longer pretend that both were possible. I had thought that I could have it all, but now I was in danger of ending up with nothing. Me or we. What would I choose?

I gulped my lager.

'Ben, I'm not coming to Antarctica.'

Ben stared out of the window, considering his words. Outside a red bus passed, glinting in the sunlight. Ben was the third person in history to ski solo to the North Pole. He was always assertive and confident when he spoke. I waited for his thoughts. But Ben just looked down and sipped his lime and soda. I filled the silence.

'I can't go on juggling two lives. It isn't fair on Sarah or Tom and Lucy.'

'I'm really sorry, Al. I felt this stuff was weighing on you.'

I just nodded. There was nothing else to say. I emptied my pint, gave Ben a hug and walked out of the pub in tears. Ben went to the South Pole, and I went to pick the kids up from nursery.

Grace

EACH TOWN HAS A vibe, and its people somehow share it. In some of the places I played, passers-by simply ignored me. But busking also depends on the attitude you project. You can fix a grin on your face but you can't fake the feeling. If I was grumpy, I had to find something to be happy about. If scared, I needed guts. If I was impatient, then patience would get me places more quickly. If someone was annoying me, I should smile at them, as I have always done to suspicious border guards and policemen.

Antonio had told me all the way back on Day One that confidence is like a board game, and urged me to roll the dice. If they land well you leap forward, buoyed with confidence. Yet that can change. An unlucky roll, a twist of fate, and you are soon crumpled back down where you began.

Today was market day. I unpacked my violin opposite an ice-cream parlour and a bookshop, a small way beyond the food and clothes stalls. I positioned my music stand in front of the bottle banks as it was in the shade. A waiter was writing the day's menu on a blackboard so I ambled across to read, and to dine vicariously.

Caldo gallego
Pimientos de Padrón
Polbo á feira
Androlla
Queso de tetilla
Tarta de Santiago

I spoke to the group of friends sitting at the café table closest to where I had set my music stand. I apologised in advance for my playing and said I would move if the noise bothered them. But they just wished me luck. When I began playing, everyone laughed. And they cheered in surprise when I received my first donation, to the embarrassment of the amorous couple who had given the coin.

While I busked, the friends enjoyed their meal, summoning the waiter repeatedly for more drinks and food. I played and played, but it was a frustrating session and I earned only pennies. After a couple of hours, the group pushed aside plates of leftovers, rose to their feet and departed. Surely, after our banter and all their fun, one of them would offer something to me? But no. They left the plaza without a word in my direction, laughing among themselves, arm in arm. Ah, but Al, nobody is obliged to you.

Twins walking towards me caught my eye, their waist-length brown hair swinging. They wore matching ripped jeans, white shirts and pink Converse trainers. They were about 20 years old, beautiful, and they knew it. One had 'Papa' tattooed on her left elbow, the other 'Mama' on her right. They ignored my playing in a way that made very clear that they had noticed me but thought me a fool.

A group of kids gathered around for a laugh. A boy flicked sunflower seeds at me. His friends guffawed. I glowered. The boy changed his mind and sloped off elsewhere for his fun.

A man sat alone with his thoughts, scrutinising the world from a café. His gelled hair shone in the sunshine. He sat stony-faced with his legs crossed, his espresso long since finished and the ashtray filling. He wore dark glasses so I could not read his eyes. I knew that he probably was not frowning at me, but it began to feel that way.

'Screw you, miserable sod,' I muttered.

Every family and couple and businessman and builder walked past as though I was not there. This town was a disaster. I was too hot to continue, but I had to. I worried that the violin would warp in the sun or the strings snap. I certainly felt warped and wobbly myself. Each tune that elicited no response from the man in the café wound me up even more. And still my nemesis did not move. He just sat with his eyes fixed on me as I sawed away. This was the last town for days. I needed to earn something. I was running out of ideas. But one thing was clear: I had to keep playing. I had to get out of this hole, and nobody else would do that for me.

In desperation, I turned to my B-list. I had been learning the tunes on it for a while, but I played these even less proficiently than the others. I could play my Top Five right the way through, sometimes even with only a couple of fluffed notes. But my B-list songs were nothing more than practice sessions in public.

Perhaps to summon help from above, I began with 'Amazing

Grace'. My pacing was terrible. I stuttered and had to start again. The stony-faced man stood up and left the café while I was trying to get the hang of the opening bars. He walked towards me. I was not in the mood for what was coming. I scowled in anticipation of his rudeness and played louder.

> T'was grace that brought us safe thus far
> And grace will lead us home.

The man drew closer and then, without speaking or looking at me, dropped two euros into my violin case. He did not even break stride. How sweet the sound of those falling coins! Whatever he had been pondering over his coffee, he was not the man I had built him up to be. I had been wretched, but he saved me.

Help

I WAS NEVER THE cleverest or quickest or most popular boy. Growing up, I always felt mediocre and on the margins. I craved recognition and success. Only when I discovered the world of endurance did I find something I could do well. I could never be the fastest, but I would not quit. I never started a fight, but nor would I lose one. You might beat me over a mile, but I'll win over a hundred. Beat me over a hundred and I'll endure for a thousand. I'll cycle across the fucking planet if I need to.

Sarah didn't care about any of this. Honey, I'm tougher than the rest, I cried, but she loved me for traits I rarely considered. For years I prided myself on being hard, a text-book defence against weakness. Fractured bones grow back stronger. There is a saying I used to love: 'Being fit is easy. It's being hard that's hard.'

Year by year, challenge by challenge, I forged myself harder than anyone I ever walked or ran or rode alongside. (I chuckle to think of a few hardy friends who will dispute this when they read it!) I made it a secret point of principle on expeditions never to give up first. Never admit weakness before someone else cracked. Cycling through Russia, my friend Rob and I continually had to ride deep into the night. We were on a ghastly 3,000-mile race against a visa deadline. The temperature had fallen to −40°, we could barely see and ice covered the trail. We skidded and crashed through the darkness. Reaching our necessary daily mileage was hell, but we could not afford to fall behind schedule. Day after day I gritted my teeth through the shivering exhaustion, pleading silently but persevering until Rob eventually buckled, dropped his laden bike in the snow, and called out in submission, 'I can't go on. Please, can we camp now?'

It was a petty and irritating trait when we should have been enjoying the bond of hardship and sharing the struggle. Cycling home from Siberia was brutal enough without me doing nothing to help or comfort Rob.

I needed to prove myself to myself all the time. Cold showers and run till you puke. In winter I flung the car windows wide open, seeing how long I could tolerate the icy wind, music blasting in the fast lane, suffering, joyful at finding something that made me different, something at last that I was good at.

But those days were past. Now the heater was on and the windows up. I drove extra slowly to delay getting home. Crying with the songs on the radio, I accepted the truth. I was not hard. I was fragile. My life was reduced to sobbing in the slow lane.

What awaited me when I steeled myself to open the front door – often after sitting outside in the dark for an hour or more – were the three people I loved the most. Yet I couldn't cope with it. A madness was crushing my mind.

Throughout these years, guilt at my feelings sharpened the

tender occasions. Watching my children in football matches, dance recitals, blowing out birthday candles: everything tore me open and brought me to tears. I was in the prime of my life but in a dark place. I had lost the right path. I started to wonder whether I even wanted to live. I needed help.

'Talk to me,' said the doctor.

I crumpled. The time had come to speak honestly and openly. I took a deep, trembling breath.

No, I am not struggling financially. Yes, all of my family are healthy. No, nobody has died. Yes, you've got that right, my job basically does involve me going on holidays and goofing around on the internet. Yep, I do actually get paid to do that. I knew that many people would envy my life. My problems were so small. I could not look the doctor in the eye. Silence. I did not know what else to say.

'Bloody hell, I'm going to be 40 next year.'

The shadow of middle age had engulfed me. I had reached the solstice, and it was downhill towards darkness from here. Halfway. Midsummer. This was my midsummer morning.

'Sit down,' said the counsellor my GP referred me to, offering the sofa. Her small room smelled of disinfectant. I sat down, my arms folded tightly across my chest, bristling. Not for the first time, I wondered what the hell had happened to my life. The humming strip light amplified our silences. I mumbled my story again, telling her about my family, those distant days of open roads, and how I just felt so sad all the time.

'I am so bored and disappointed with my life.'

'Why?' asked Holly, smiling. 'And what are you going to do about it?'

And so began a series of irritatingly, amusingly combative sessions.

'I am wasting my best years. I can't do what I love anymore.'

'Why?'

'Because I have a wife and two kids and I can no longer chase life.'

'You could leave. Why don't you?'

I saw what answers Holly was guiding me towards. I knew they made sense. But I wriggled and argued with all my might. I did not want to concede. I wanted to cling to the strange comfort of blame and regret. But patiently, persistently, Holly wore me down and helped me regain some perspective on my life. She logically and calmly disarmed my fury by holding up a mirror to show me what I already knew was there. She showed me my self-pity.

'Why don't I go on expeditions anymore?' I answered. 'Because I have to look after my children.'

'Why?'

It was like arguing with a 2-year-old, albeit a canny and well-paid one. I sighed and relented. It was almost a relief to do so.

'Because, faced with the choice of staying or going, I want to be here.'

'Why?'

'Because my family are the most rewarding thing I've ever known. I love them more than anything.'

Choices

ALL OF MY LIFE was my choice. I chose to get married and become a father. I can never go back on that. Nor would I want to. I chose not to walk away. I was, I realised belatedly, living the life of my choice. It was up to me what I chose to make of it now.

I began to look for adventure closer to home, searching for opportunities rather than groaning at the limitations. I taught myself to find short, local escapes compatible with the constraints of real life. I called them microadventures. Sleeping on a hill is no big deal, but it gave me a little hit of what I was missing. A sip of espresso is not a large latte, but it tastes similar and gives you a buzz. A little adventure is better than no adventure. The ideas behind these overnight escapes spread to others, and I wrote a book about them. I discovered that there were many people dreaming of adventure but struggling to make it happen.

Microadventures helped restore my sanity, providing a dose of wilderness, offline stillness and physical toil, but still getting me back home in time to do the school run. Hearing about other people getting out on microadventures of their own made me feel better still.

Fast-forward a while and the exhausting nappy years were finally behind us. The tension, point-scoring and bickering receded. Tom and Lucy made me laugh every day. My heart swelled every time they sought out my lap to curl up for a cuddle. I adored the silliness of our antics: the Garden World Cup penalty shootouts, dancing to YouTube girl bands and play fights on the sofa. The moment I let go of the saddle and watched them pedal off on their bikes in perfect freedom trumped any ride of my own. Their own adventures have begun.

Slowly I began removing the wedge I had hammered between Sarah and me. I had battered it in hard over years of stubborn fury, with my seething silences and moping lassitude. I started to work it free, remembering why I loved Sarah and trying to become grateful and kind once again. The wound, Rumi said, is the place where the light enters you. I had numbed many of my vulnerabilities to help me cope, but doing so had muted everything, including my joys. I gradually let go of who I used to be, or thought I should be, and began unpicking who I was now.

Sarah and I regained some of our own lives, her with her career and me with my microadventures. I was proud when Sarah returned home one evening and announced she had won a hard-earned promotion. She was flying. I encouraged her to spend more time in the garden she loves, and to go out more with her friends. Helping Sarah live a full life makes me happier.

But then, perhaps inevitably, the prospect of one more trip

started glimmering in the back of my mind. I had hoped I might have left those dreams behind. I had tried so hard to stop considering expeditions. Our lives were far simpler without them. But, I began to reflect, something might be possible now without putting too much burden on the family. I knew I could not have Laurie's endless summer. Those days were past and at last I accepted that. Perhaps, though, I could get one final chance to say goodbye to those days. Our life was running reasonably smoothly, but on a personal level I still felt frustrated and unfulfilled. I still craved to be living adventurously, not just retelling the same old stories to pay the bills.

We talked, and Sarah and I decided that a month-long journey was workable. It was selfish of me, but she was willing for me to go, kind as always. Tom and Lucy would miss me, and I would be sad to leave them. But, in my own muddled way, I needed to do this for them. I wanted, above all else in life, to be a good dad. That was more important than any adventure or ambition. I needed to show my children what I believed in. I hoped to instil a love of the outdoors, insist they pay attention to being alive, encourage them to seize their lives and opportunities, and to be curious, wild and bold.

I wanted Tom and Lucy to see that there are so many possible paths in life, like the mesh of animal tracks fanning out from a waterhole. They can pick a less trodden path if they wish, or even forge their own. They do not have to follow the route prescribed by school and society. But if they do pick that well-trodden path, then it must be a deliberate decision. I had to teach them that they too have a choice.

But I had to show them this way of life, not just preach it.

Stuck at home, I was not setting an example I was proud of. I needed to become the man I wanted Tom and Lucy to know.

Above my desk is this quote from Jung. I look at it every day: 'The life that I could still live, I should live, and the thoughts that I could still think, I should think.'

I went out and bought a violin.

Fear

THESE THINGS FRIGHTEN ME:

- Looking a fool.
- Relying upon busking for money.
- Turning 40 next year.
- My next decade will be less interesting than my thirties.
- My thirties were less exciting than my twenties.
- Becoming weaker and slower every year.
- Relying on the past for my identity: my old stories are my best stories.
- Failing to fulfil my potential and wasting my life.
- Marriage becoming a disappointment and my wife and I growing apart.
- Not raising my children to be wild, bold and curious.
- Never being as happy as someone so fortunate as me ought to be.

In other words: don't fear the violin.
Perspective is handy, my friend!

Casting

I NEVER WANTED TO play my violin, but I wanted to have played. That was enough to make me do it. Every time I picked up the instrument I was more experienced, a little better, a little less uncertain. This helped me creep towards confidence. Yet surely my luck would desert me? I would be unmasked as the foolish Emperor, shooed out of town for fiddling in his preposterous new clothes, naked and hungry in a foreign land. But, in town after town, nobody minded me turning up and playing. I never banished the fear, but I learned to do it anyway. With time, I even grew to enjoy the whole performance and find it hilarious.

Watching loot pile up in my violin case, I was astonished to be earning enough to live on. I had become a professional musician! Granted, I was a musician with a repertoire of five short songs, performed poorly. But some days I even earned more than three euros! I could dine like a king. Busking is the most exhilarating way I have ever made a living. It was so unpredictable, uplifting and – frankly – undeserved. There was no sensible reason for anyone to give me money: you can listen to the best music in the world for free. My playing was rubbish and money is tight in Spain these days. The cash was pure kindness. Every time someone gave me a coin they unknowingly invested in my journey, feeding me, making me feel less alone.

Busking is like fishing. Not all rivers, not all streets, are equal. You must choose your place carefully to hook people. Pick up your violin and tune her. Cast well, and play with soul to reel them in, whether you're a dab hand or fresh out of school. Play Schubert's Quintet in A major, work your scales. Persevere, do not flounder.

The performance is your bait. But your eyes are the hook. Eye contact is critical in busking. Catch someone's gaze and you're halfway to catching a coin. Of course, as any fisherman knows, the fish can still twist free. You cannot relax until it's on the bank and the coin is in the case. Strike prematurely, catching the eye of a pedestrian when he is too far away, and he has time to look elsewhere and swerve course. Strike too late, meet eyes when she is too near, and momentum will carry your fish by before she feels the twinge of guilt or spark of connection and reaches for her money. Your slender line snaps.

A proficient busker's tools consist therefore of musical ability, location, the bait of a tune and the hook of eye contact. But I had no skill, rotten bait, and needed to concentrate too hard to look around much. When I did glance up from my music sheets, hoping for sympathy, I often lost my place and stumbled.

But all it ever required was a little flick of a coin for someone to end the nagging worry of my next meal. This is why fly fishing is more intriguing than darts. One requires dexterity and skill, repeated over and over again. The other demands skill, plus many nuances, plus a slice of luck. When it all comes together, the surprise and thrill is electric.

Back in England, I had doubted whether my plan was possible for a novice violinist. My friends agreed. Why not delay a year until you are competent, they suggested? Or at least permit yourself a spending allowance, just in case? You'll still play the violin; you'll still do the walk. It will be more realistic, more achievable, that's all.

These were pragmatic, well-meaning suggestions, but I pushed them away. A daily stipend would have diluted everything. The insecurity of needing to busk was what made the journey. Had I carried a cushion of money, the music would have become nothing but a game or an affectation. Instead, it was my work, and it was critical. That made all the difference. I earned these coins. By the sweat of my face, I earned this bread. I earned these miles.

One Day

MOST DAYS IN SPAIN I walked beyond the horizon, 20 miles or more. Ferreras de Arriba, Sarracín de Aliste, Riofrío de Aliste . . . The villages came and went, but I remember the discomfort. Gravel tracks, sharp underfoot, stretching ahead until they melted into a pale horizon beneath a vast blue sky flecked with clouds. I remember the heat, my nose and lips burning and splitting. And I remember day after day alone with my thoughts. The percussive chirp of insects in dusty bushes, lilac and scraggy like heather. Green kilometre markers counting down the approach to towns. Raising a hiking pole to wave at drivers. Shouting a brief explanation to inquisitive workmen tiling a roof. A soulless village with heaps of rubble on the pavement, garage doors hanging off hinges, but a shaded *pelota* wall to rest against.

I remember the dragging hours of busking. Pausing between songs to stretch my back, shift my weight from leg to leg, and summon the resolve to play again. Everything hard: the ground, the light, earning money.

I remember food. Watching a child eating *tortilla* with oily fingers, tipping back his head to fit the slice into his mouth, golden egg and potato spilling wasted onto the pavement. I saw a painter crack open a boiled egg with his brush handle and craved eggs for days afterwards.

It is important on a journey to grind out these slow, unremarkable miles. They heft you to the landscape and the moods of future joys, the hardship building the soundtrack to your unique journey and the new poetry of your life.

I appreciated the slowness of walking in a fast world. It is the ancient way of travel, and even technology cannot help. Only persistence and effort make an impact. It is easy to begin but hard to stick at, which is why I respect anyone who has completed a long hike. You learn a lot about someone by hiking in the hills.

Writing now, I must try to lay down the ambient background of slowness, heat and modest but constant pain. Too loud and you will tire of the moaning. Too soft and you miss a critical dimension. Plug away, plod away, drift away. Time does the rest, turning a walk into something richer, as cream changes to golden butter under duress. Though individual days blend together, the result becomes an experience more vibrant than the mere cumulative act of trudging towards the next sit-down and sandwich. Travel long and slow and you learn to pay attention.

Time moves strangely on the road: at once fast and slow. There is real time, told by tolling church towers and the sun's relentless sweep. But there is also walking time, marked by the body and mind – tortured soles and souls – that pays scant heed to the chronological order of the universe. Weeks fly, days pass, hours and minutes drag: just me, my violin and my shadow slowly crossing the landscape with Laurie. 'The days,' he wrote, 'merged into a continuous movement of sun and shadow, hunger and thirst, fatigue and sleep, all fused and welded into one coloured mass by the violent heat of that Spanish summer.' This is just one day of my life. But every day to come will depend fractionally on what I do today. I must live it as vividly as I can bear to do.

My spirits soared on peaceful forest tracks as I stepped back into the same landscapes that Laurie encountered, the sounds and pace matching his experience. Only a jay noticed me, rasping its alarmed cry through the oak trees with a flash of white tail. I pushed through blackberry brambles, an all-you-can-eat buffet come autumn, but there was no fruit yet and so only their thorns delayed me, snatching at my clothes and pack. Escaping into a clearing, I came upon a stream and a trout-ringed pool. Emerald pondweed swayed in the deep, and the water reflected white clouds and blue sky. Butterflies danced and the air smelled of summer grass. I tore off my shirt.

'Fwah! Fwah! Fwah!' I gasped as I jumped into the pool, the international language of cold water on hot days, and the only sound beneath the sweep of wind in the trees.

Seconds later I was out again, sloshing waves with my bullish exit. I pulled on my trousers and was dripping like a dog in the sunshine when an old farmer passed through the woods. He was carrying a wooden rake over his shoulder, on his way to turn the drying hay in his field. His face was soft and his dark hair lay flat like a bowl. He chuckled at my shivers.

'We used to swim here as children, ten or twelve of us playing all summer. All of *la comunidad* shares this pool,' he said. 'We have always swum here, our friends. It hasn't changed much around here in all my life.'

I loved the notion of a community pool and consecutive generations coming to enjoy it.

I urged myself to swim a second time, to relish the sensation of being cold. All day I had complained and struggled against the heat. I shouldn't then abandon its opposite so readily. On walks what you face right now is often hard. Too hot, too cold, too tired, too hungry. The lazy brain cries out for something different and yearns for elsewhere. But I needed to stop pining. Enjoy now for what it is. Suck the goodness from today, for it too will pass.

I leapt back in to the pool, holding my breath underwater and enjoying the dimmed translucence of the sunlight, the burn of the cold water on my body.

Lost

MY RUCKSACK BOUNCED ON my shoulders as I marched down a steep and winding hill, congratulating myself on relaxing from my usual obsessive map checking. Unshackled from that worry, I strode forwards, head up, breathing in the vistas that stretched away across mountains covered with gum trees and pine.

The jumbled villages hinted at a subsistence pace of life little changed since Laurie passed through, 'places of steep craggy lanes and leaf-smothered towers and old doors pitted with gigantic keyholes'. I walked among gardens heaving with glossy aubergines, tomatoes and golden courgette flowers. Simple stone cottages lined the lane. I heard dogs and cockerels, smelled the jasmine that arched over doorways and greeted bearded old women carrying pails to the *fuente*. They dressed in pinafores and wellies with headscarves tied under the chin, chewed their gums and glowered at me.

An hour later I reached the valley floor. A pretty young woman stopped her car and asked me for directions. She had taken her granny for an afternoon drive, but got lost. I whipped open my map with an eager flourish to impress, rescued her and sent them on their way. Noticing, as I did so, that I had come the wrong way myself.

I waited until the woman's car was out of sight. Then I turned around and stomped back up the bloody mountain the way I had come. My only consolation were the bewildered faces of old women, half certain they had seen somebody very similar – only smilier – passing in the other direction.

In softer evening light I veered off the footpath and got lost again. This time I was content to follow my nose wherever it led. So long as I followed my shadow I knew I was going roughly the right way. I hummed as I passed through the clumpy grass and thistles of sheep fields alongside a tiny water channel. Who had dug this ditch? How long had it flowed? Was I the first foreigner to pass this way? It seemed unlikely, given the millennia of invaders and merchants and tourists who have tramped across Spain. But it was fun to imagine I was blazing my own trail.

Getting back on course required a few exhausting minutes of ploughing through bushes, followed by a tricky stream crossing. Grabbing handfuls of spiky branches, I heaved myself through a thicket of Spanish broom, tangled amongst the gaudy yellow flowers and sweet vanilla perfume. I paused at the stream, considering whether I could jump it. I decided not to risk it. Instead I teetered across from boulder to boulder.

'If the violin gets wet, the trip is over,' I cautioned myself out loud, over and over. 'Fall here, and it's the end.'

It was a tiny incident, short enough to be entertaining, hard enough to cause me to puff my cheeks with relief when it was over. No big deal. But as I scrabbled, scratched and itching, back onto the path, I reflected how small mistakes on adventures can escalate into significant problems in a way I rarely encounter at home. Slipping on a rock and breaking your ankle would be unfortunate wherever it occurred. But the prospect of it happening miles from a road focuses the mind. Nobody would report me missing for weeks, a reminder that everything out here was my responsibility. Expeditions force me to hold up an unforgiving mirror – often when I am tired, ruffled, and not at my best. There is nowhere to hide. The enforced honesty of travel is sobering but liberating.

Rhythm

I HAD SETTLED NOW into the rhythm of the journey. Waking at dawn, walking through forests, ploughing across hillsides of gorse and bracken, seeking water and conversation in villages. Hoping to busk. Hustling for a crust. Idyllic days of butterfly meadows sprayed with buttercups and cow parsley, clover and dandelions, velvety bentgrass and cuckooflower, knapweed and ribwort. My feet and ankles wet with dew. The hum of bees and the smell of honeysuckle. Even Laurie would not need to exaggerate such abundance with his notoriously purple prose.

Slad-like villages – slow, out-of-the-way places – gushed with white streams that gambolled like lambs beside the cobbled lanes. There were fountains and troughs for both man and beast, and watermills that once ground flour. In one village, a stream flowed directly through the *fuente*, beneath an old stone cross and down past the church. Old folk traipsed to it along the alley to fill buckets for their gardens, carrying them on yokes across their shoulders.

I followed winding byways between villages, grassy

underfoot and lined with foxgloves, blackberries, heather and expansive views. Around mid-morning I lay under a tree to rest. The grass, still shaded, was cool and moist beneath me. 'Sometimes I'd hide from the sun under the wayside poplars, face downwards watching the ants,' Laurie wrote. 'There was really no hurry. I was going nowhere. Nowhere at all but here.' Dappled sunlight dazzled through the swaying leaves, pools of light danced on my closed eyelids, and I dozed for deep, groggy minutes. I shocked myself awake with a paddle in a chilly stream, lush with green reeds and iridescent blue dragonflies. The stream bed's smooth pebbles massaged the soles of my feet.

How frequently I busked depended upon the spacing of communities along the way. I wanted to play every day, but sometimes two or three fallow days would pass. I had to stretch my supplies accordingly, imposing rationing when I was worried. The prospect of carrot sandwiches was ample motivation to walk faster or busk longer! As soon as I earned some money I headed to the nearest shop or market stall to replenish my supplies. On days when I earned little I concentrated on buying food that would fill my belly. This always included a fresh loaf. If I had a successful day – more than three euros, say – then I gave thought to a more balanced diet, scanning the shelves for cheap fruit and vegetables, peanuts, or tins of lentils and sardines.

My alarm woke me at the same time each day. Over the weeks I noticed the creeping delay of dawn as the season moved on. Walking offers the space and time to grow aware of subtle changes in nature as a journey unfolds. I observed whether today was warmer or cloudier than yesterday. It mattered here. Or which direction the wind was blowing. The carried sounds changed: a distant motorway from a northerly, church bells if it backed to the east. I appreciated nights with a light breeze to wick away sweat and deter mosquitoes. I had no mosquito repellent so relied hopelessly on adopting a Zen-like indifference to that ghastly whine. On still nights I also woke soaked with dew. But too much wind meant I slept cold, waking after a few hours to put on my raincoat, pulling the hood up for a little more warmth, and curling into a ball. The moon shrank night by night, and I watched it set in the southwest almost an hour later each day. I measured my trip by its size. The next time the moon was full, I calculated, my walk would nearly be over.

Was this how Laurie experienced Spain all those years ago? Many aspects of a long walk and a foreign adventure never change. Even today there were only a few glimpses of modernity: the power lines curving across valleys and the cars parked outside homes. The acceleration in transport speed was perhaps the most significant change between my Spain and Laurie's, for the way it compresses distances and draws people and ideas closer together. Compare my occasional reluctant marches down busy roads with the pace of Laurie's Spain when he walked 'slightly faster than the mule-trains strung along the route, though slower than trotting asses. On these straight Spanish roads, so empty of motor cars, we moved between horizons like ships at sea, often remaining for hours within sight of each other, gradually losing or gaining ground . . . a rhythm unchanged since the days of Hannibal.'

Baggage

EVERYTHING I OWNED, I carried. On my back, I carried a blue 48-litre rucksack. The lightweight straps sliced into my shoulders. I had dreamed of a respite from the agonies of overloaded expedition packs on this simple, warm walk. But I had underestimated the amount of camera equipment I would carry, so the pack was crammed irritatingly full, and I regretted it was not larger. The cover of *As I Walked Out One Midsummer Morning* shows Laurie barefoot, carrying a small bundle under his arm. This romanticised notion of minimalist travel appealed, though I knew Laurie had actually carried a knapsack. I now carried a gnawing worry that Laurie's golden yarn of a carefree, vagabond journey might not match the reality of trudging hungry through a Spanish summer, crushed beneath a heavy pack.

The battered 1974 Penguin edition of the book I carried is a slim volume, just 186 pages. Its spine was cracked and bound with sellotape, my name scribbled on the endpaper in a younger man's handwriting. Every night I unpacked the book and a diary from the rucksack. As my notebook's empty pages filled with my hasty, messy hand, what began as Laurie's story slowly became our story. In the pouch at the back of the diary, I carried three yellow Post-it Notes from my family. One bore a drawing from Lucy: a stick person with two legs, long hair and two dots for eyes. No arms, nose or mouth. The picture from Tom was a smiling stick figure two years more proficient. And on the third, from Sarah, a simple heart scribbled blue by – I guessed – Lucy.

Inside the back cover of the diary I made a chart with two columns, recording how much I earned each day and my accumulated total. The list began with smug satisfaction:

Day 1: €4. Total earnings: €4

Inside the rucksack, I carried my home. A sleeping bag, 473 grams of goose down, sensuously flimsy in my hands. I carried a silk liner to slip inside for a little more warmth on cold nights, as a refreshing alternative on hot nights, and for a valuable illusion of luxury when I lay unwashed on flinty ground, cushioned only by 408 grams of foam sleeping mat. I took to folding the silver and yellow mat into a Z-shape, sacrificing some length for a small midsection of triple thickness where my bony hips pressed into the earth. The foam was thin, but when I lay on it and took my 85 kilograms of weight (80 kilograms after a month) off my feet, it was a moment in heaven.

I carried a red tarpaulin, 300 grams of caution, in case of rain. I carried lengths of string and four pegs, 96 grams, to rig the tarp into a shelter. In this way I also carried reassurance.

I carried a small titanium pan, 94 grams, that offered almost a litre of eating capacity – this being approximately the volume of a happily-full stomach. I carried a flint to spark my cooking fires, preferring a fire's zero grams of heat and light and company to the weight and expense of a stove and fuel. I knew I carried the burden of responsibility for bringing fire into Spain's dry forests, but I trusted my skills.

I carried a baby's plastic spoon to eat with and a head torch for light. I carried whatever food my busking earned me, feast or famine as fate decreed. I carried a 10-litre water bag so that even in the driest landscapes I could roam free like a camel. Empty, the bag was tiny; full it was bloated and heavy. I also carried a two-litre drinking bladder with a long straw that dangled over my shoulder from my rucksack. Even in the hottest, driest, poorest places I have been in the world, water is always given freely.

I carried hiking poles, 266 grams each, to help my knees bear the load, and to give rhythm to my pace. I wore trainers, socks, trousers, a belt and a long shirt. I could roll up my shirt sleeves and unbutton the front if I was hot. The trousers zipped into shorts. A versatile item is worth its weight in gold in the outdoors. Indeed, it is more precious than that, for gold is worthless to a hungry, tired man. I began the trip wearing boxer shorts but soon discarded them for being hot and uncomfortable. Judge me not: I carried only useful weight! At evening camps, I sometimes emptied my pack on the ground and pared away a couple of surplus items – my spare pen, a map I had finished with. This saved only a few grams, but the psychological boost of knowing I carried only what I needed was satisfying.

I carried a long-sleeved base layer to sleep in rather than my sweat-soaked shirt, a versatile tube balaclava and a second pair of socks. My most precious tool was not only my violin but also my walking feet. They deserved pampering with the extravagance of spare socks.

Pale-skinned, I shied from the heat with a sun hat and sunglasses. I also carried a light raincoat: I am too English to go anywhere without suspecting rain. It never rained. There's a lesson in there, somewhere.

Bungeed to my rucksack, along with the sleeping mat, I carried my violin case. It was on the outside for two reasons: the instrument was too bulky to fit inside, but I also snobbishly hoped it would differentiate me from a 'mere' hiker, backpacker or – God forbid – 'tourist', and thus people might respond more warmly to me.

My violin was varnished spruce and maple, 60 centimetres long and just 440 grams. I admired the robust curve of its waist, the sinuous scroll and f-holes, and the tactile tuning pegs. I carried a bow, 75 centimetres of smooth brazilwood and taut horsehair, rubbed with rosin. And I carried spare strings, a small electric tuner to aid my ignorant ear, a music stand, sheet music and a couple of clothes pegs to hold the pages in place.

Laurie would have understood most of the things I carried. We had much that was similar, though he carried some items I did not: a tent, a blanket, a supply of money, a change of clothes, thick boots, a hazel stick, a tin of treacle biscuits and some cheese. What would have been alien to Laurie were all the electronics I carried and the annoying tagalong gubbins needed to charge them. The irony of lugging kilograms of expensive cameras to document a minimalist, penniless adventure did not pass unnoticed or uncursed. But I love filming and photography, and the creative side of adventuring has become integral to the whole experience for me.

I carried spares and repairs. Zinc oxide tape to protect my feet where they rubbed, Vaseline to soothe chafing parts and Ibuprofen to forget pains. I carried a length of gaffer tape wrapped around my spare pen, a needle threaded with a couple of metres of dental floss for sewing repairs, a tiny penknife, toilet paper, sun cream, toothbrush and toothpaste. I carried maps and a compass, more from habit than necessity, for I also carried my phone. It held not only the entirety of human knowledge but also – more useful to me – hiking maps so that I could walk most of the way off-road. Uncomfortable with taking a smartphone on a simple walk, I deleted the music, email and apps, and banned myself from the internet. We have grown addicted to being in constant contact with the world and lost the gift of being disconnected.

On top of all this gear, I carried many more things in my head. Harder to measure in grams, but they weighed heavy or light upon me. This baggage accounted for many of the reasons I was here in Spain. I carried memories and experience from all my years of taking journeys, and my hopes for this new one. This confidence and anticipation was a pleasure and a privilege that sat lightly and lifted me. I carried curiosity, stamina and a reluctant willingness to look stupid.

I carried memories of my family, my love for them and their love for me. I carried sadness and guilt about leaving them behind and the weight of too many occasions when 'adventure' had, in truth, meant 'running away'.

I carried years of regrets and resentments – far too many. They are heavy and worthless to carry. This walk was an opportunity to sift through them all. I wanted to jettison them here in Spain and replace them with the lightness of hope. Hope for my children's lives, hope for my marriage and hope that this trip might help turn my life around and move us all on to less tempestuous times.

On top of everything else, I carried the love of my wife. I thought of her delicate bones when I held Sarah's hand or wrapped my arms around her, such strength in one small body. I pictured her sleeping face among the pillows, and the way she wrinkles her nose to guffaw at her own jokes. I carried her kindness, good sense and patient loyalty. I have carried Sarah's love for almost half my life, even during the times when I forgot I had it and it was her love carrying me.

And so I carried into Spain a determination to change my life, for, despite everything that had happened in recent years, I loved my family deeply and did not want to lose them.

Quite a load to bear for one man and his rucksack, alone in the hills of Galicia.

First Light

THINK OF MORNING ON a long walk as the period
that flows on from the night rather than a discrete new start.
A day on the trail runs more neatly from evening to evening
than morning to morning. Setting up camp marks the end
of a day, and afterwards something new begins. The more
of a trip you spend continually outdoors – day to day, week
to month – the deeper the experience becomes. Laurie also
appreciated the rapture of first light: 'When I awoke the
next morning it was already light . . . and I was heavily
drenched in dew. I wriggled out of the blanket, crawled onto
the ridge, and lay in the rising sun . . . I felt it was for this
I had come; to wake at dawn on a hillside and look out on
a world for which I had no words, to start at the beginning,
speechless and without plan, in a place that still had no
memories for me.'

I followed my nose towards a village bakery. It was closed.
I pushed the door and it swung open. I stepped inside.

'*¿Hola?*' I called into the gloom. My mouth watered at the
aroma of fresh bread. I waited, then shouted again, a little

louder this time. After a minute a stout woman appeared, rolling like a ship. Bandages bound her swollen ankles.

'*¡Buenos días!* Please can I buy a loaf? I slept in the hills last night and I'm hungry.'

'It will be ready soon. You can come in and wait.'

It was mid-morning and yet they were only just baking the day's first loaves. My father, a baker himself, would have preferred the Spanish schedule to his years of pre-dawn starts! Here the horn of the baker's van, tooting around villages for lunch business, was often the first loud noise of the day, an alarm clock for laid-back Spain.

I followed the lady through a door. The smells of flour dust and heat conjured childhood memories of my dad's bakery. The baker was keeping a careful eye on his loaves through the oven window, occasionally shoving wedges of wood into the flames below. He nodded a friendly greeting. They were a pleasant, placid couple. I had disturbed their routine, getting in the way and throwing a hundred questions into what I imagined was usually an amiable, well-rehearsed silence. I learned that they baked 360 loaves a day, more at the weekends and on holidays, and had done so daily for 40 years.

'That's a lot of bread! That's longer than I have been alive.'

I bought the first loaf out of the oven and tore it to pieces, hot and moist, as I walked. A red kite circled on rising thermals, also hungry, wings spread as it rose, forked tail translucent when it passed across the sun. The hunter carried an air of menace, even to me, the only species that bird ever has to fear.

I stopped to prepare a banana sandwich. On my tight budget, eating two different food items simultaneously felt hedonistic. My body craved the sweetness of banana with the fierce appreciation of flavour that comes when you exercise a lot. Laurie described living 'on pressed dates and biscuits, rationing them daily, as though crossing a desert'. I turned to look at the landscape I had crossed. So many other travelling days have begun this way. Roadside banana sandwiches. Flinging pebbles at signposts, cheering the clang of success. Making deals about how much longer I'd allow myself to sit. Five more cars, then I'll get going. OK, maybe another five. One more strike of the signpost. One more banana sandwich.

I wish I could bottle the early happiness of the road, the day not yet hot, feet not sore, brain not riled. Birds and bees the only sound, and as I walked my head buzzed with enthusiasm. I peered into the distance, scanning for clues for how far away the next village might be. I was eager to busk again, to try my luck in a new town with a new audience. Even on the days filled with setbacks, busking was exciting. I felt better than I had done for years. I was exercising hard with the warm sun on my face. I was slimmer and stronger, living simply and with purpose. In a few weeks, I would be with my family again, and I was looking forward to that, too. Feeling this way was a joyful epiphany. Morning is always my most positive time of day. The scale of the challenges ahead looks enticing rather than intimidating.

Buscando

THE ENGLISH WORD 'BUSK' derives from the Spanish verb *buscar*: to seek. What was I seeking out in Spain with my violin? Certainly not fame and fortune. I was grubby and hungry, sweating in the dirt, listening to the mad meanderings of my mind. If anything, I was trying to stop seeking. To be still, and to become content. I had not been happy for years.

Back home, time is my most scarce and precious commodity. The shortness of life distresses me. So I try to squeeze too much into too little time, ending up wildly busy or seething with frustration. For too long this drove me to mania as I tried to cram full my life. One wedding anniversary I gave Sarah a necklace hung with a tiny hourglass. Tip it, and the sand flows through. Past, present and future: all visible at the same time.

'This is all our times together,' I told Sarah. 'The memories we have, this day now, and all the good times still to come.'

But I could not stop myself adding, 'And to remember how fast it passes.'

Yet now I dozed beneath a tree, watching the swifts, and

allowed enchantment into my day. I was learning to let days stretch out long and slow, for 24 hours to be ample, and to allow my mind to lie fallow, far from deadlines and self-inflicted agonies. I had not brought any new books to read or music to listen to. I had nothing but time. So scarce at home, so bountiful here that I wallowed in a surfeit. I had no jobs to do except to walk and to busk. Wilfully inviting in boredom gave my brain the freedom to wander where it wondered.

I wanted to learn – somewhat late – to enjoy today more than the thought of yesterday or tomorrow. It was time to recalibrate, to savour all I had rather than mourning what was missing. Satisfaction comes, literally, from appreciating that you have enough. Use the hours, don't count them, counselled old sundials engraved with reminders of mortality. *Utere, non numera*. Neither this walk nor my life at home needed to be the sufferfest I used to pride myself upon, demanding ever more from myself, chastising myself at each finish line that I had not made it harder to reach.

I had come to Spain to learn to wear time lightly. Laurie was teaching me to treasure days rather than wringing my hands at their passing. Make haste, but slowly, is sound advice for a long journey. My life will be long enough if I use it well. *Sic labitur ætas*. Thus passes a lifetime.

Manna

I SPOTTED A CHERRY on the ground, fallen or flung from a vehicle. I smiled at my luck and groaned beneath my pack as I bent, picked it up and carried on walking. Free food! I was too conscious of the fragility of my economics to pass such gifts, even if it broke my rhythm and made my knees creak.

Distances stretch when you are walking. One hundred metres becomes a long way. Time draws out, even as the mind contracts to the horizon or the roadside flotsam. I polished the cherry on my trousers, popped it in my mouth and chewed. I savoured the fruit's sweetness, its juiciness, its glorious free-ness. Then I rolled the stone around with my tongue, sucking a poor man's gobstopper until I tired of it. Finally, I spat it into the air in front of me and volleyed it, Messi-like, against a road sign, anticipating the satisfying 'ding' as it struck. But I missed, not only the sign but the cherry stone, too.

How many calories did the fruit give? Maybe three? What distance would those calories convert to? How far had I walked as I sucked the stone and dreamed of scoring goals? I glanced back over my shoulder. About 50 metres. But then there were also the bonus yards, the mental ramblings spinning onwards after the cherry had gone, these dumb calculations. By the time that thread of thought faded away, I was a further 50 metres down the road, with the lorries and cars roaring by and an awkward camber that hurt my knees.

Later, I found a sweet. Unwrapped it and ate it. Cola flavour. Another occasion, a ketchup sachet. It was delicious – sweet and salty – as I squeezed it into my mouth. And always the road called me on, and step by step, mile by mile, song by song, the days passed.

Health Check

HARD-WON EXPERIENCE HAS TAUGHT me which parts of my feet rub raw on long hikes. At the start of a journey, I tape these spots to prevent blisters. By the time the tape falls off, my feet have toughened to their task and won't cause problems again.

Anxiety about a possible broken bone was more serious than blister worries. A few months ago, I had injured my foot in an enthusiastic but incompetent (future epitaph) taekwondo scrap with a punchbag. The punchbag won. At a family barbecue, an orthopaedic surgeon licked his fingers clean then twisted sufficient yelps from me to declare it probably broken. But nothing showed on an X-ray. So I limped towards Spain, annoyed at losing fitness, and worrying that a heavy rucksack on rocky paths was asking for trouble. So far, it was coping, though if I stumbled, sharp pains shot through the foot.

Walking uphill had hurt my hips since I crossed the Empty Quarter four years earlier. I'm getting old, I laughed as I hauled my creaking body up from the hard ground each morning. The sun cracked my lips, and I even considered forfeiting some food money on an exceptional busking day to buy lip balm. I had investigated the cost and been mulling over the decision for some time.

The laden pack bruised my shoulders. Beneath the straps, a heat rash flourished. My chest had burned into an angry red 'V', stencilled by my shirt, ludicrous against the white of my ribs and stomach. But, generally, I was in decent shape and enjoying the sensation of repeated physical effort. My leg muscles grew crisply defined, and I punched a new, tighter hole in my belt. For Laurie, this conditioning period was a satisfying part of his rite of passage. 'At first I'd hobbled, but my blisters had hardened and at last I could walk without pain. I developed a long loping stride which covered some twenty miles a day, an easy monotonous pace.'

I was in an unusually healthy frame of mind. I still wanted to walk far. I wanted to be tired and to test myself. But for the first time ever I did not feel guilty or weak when I chose not to destroy myself. I was almost becoming a reasonable person!

Bravery

THESE THINGS I HAVE done. Some people consider them brave:

- Cycling through the Middle East.
- Living for a year in a village in Africa.
- Packrafting on Iceland's torrential Þjórsá river.
- Diving beneath the ice of the frozen Arctic Ocean.
- Walking alone across southern India.
- Rowing the Atlantic.
- Attempting to make a living without a proper job.
- Bungee jumping, sky diving, swimming in the River Thames, sleeping by the HOLLYWOOD sign.

I chose eagerly to do every one.

These things I have also done. I struggled with the leap for each one. I consider them the bravest things of all:

- Getting married.
- Having children.
- Signing a mortgage.
- Playing my violin in a Spanish plaza.

Privilege

La cucaracha, la cucaracha,
Ya no puede caminar.
Porque no tiene, porque le falta
Una pata de atrás.

The cockroach, the cockroach,
Cannot walk.
Because he doesn't have, because he is missing
a hind leg.

I wish I could have played my jauntiest number, 'La Cucaracha', for Laurie. It would have reminded him of a girl (as, I suspect, would many songs). Laurie met Consuelo on his walk, though her strict Catholic parents forbade them from speaking. But Consuelo somehow slipped Laurie a note, a poem penned to the tune of 'La Cucaracha'.

Tall compared to a poor stunted fisherman,
Blond and handsome and slim,

Is a boy who arrived
To play the violin
In the Hotel Mediterráneo.
He is called Lorenzo.

Decades later, Laurie recalled, 'I've adored her for ever. Her voluptuous face and huge dark eyes still haunt me. Consuelo is still one of my favourite names.'

I played 'La Cucaracha' outside a twelfth-century Romanesque church. A dozen pensioners sat on a low wall in front of the graceful, double-arched door. They occasionally leaned on walking frames, heaved themselves to their feet and tossed me coppers for sporting effort.

Once I had earned some money, I headed down the busy shopping street to find a bakery, my shoes and ankles dusty from the morning's hike. The number of homeless people saddened me. There were far more than in a comparable town in Britain. Eighty years ago 'beggars were everywhere, sitting propped against walls' and 'sleeping out in the gutters under a coating of disease and filth' as Spain teetered towards civil war following the Great Depression. Today, some of the men and women holding out their hands or a paper cup were immigrants, washed up by the sad circumstances of their homeland, far from where they wanted their lives to be. But most were Spaniards, slouched with blank eyes, the fallout from a disastrous economy. When I played again, I took care to busk a fair distance away from them, conscious neither to encroach on their patch, nor equate their needs with my frivolities. We were both panning for kindness from strangers. Me, for amusement. Them, for survival.

The homeless made me guilty about what I was doing. I had

a home and an income, but I was pretending to be poor. In doing so, I competed for the same scraps as them. Could I justify this? Not really. I did not give my morning's earnings to one of them, for example. I regret that. Laurie once bought 'some cool, light sandals, and picked out a beggar on whom to bestow my boots'. He was accustomed in that era to seeing many people in the same predicament back home, 'that host of unemployed who wandered aimlessly about England at that time . . . They were like a broken army walking away from a war, cheeks sunken, eyes dead with fatigue.'

There was a subtle but important line that I hope spared me from being an affluent panhandler. I played for hours and never asked for anything. Because I was hopeless, I know I depended on goodwill. My 'music' did not deserve money, but I believe my effort counted for something. I was one of the lucky ones: I had a job and the opportunity to earn. I had my violin.

My heightened awareness of the way people behave – avoiding eye contact, swerves of direction – suggested my morning had been more profitable than it was for many of the homeless, even the young woman with the puppy and the sign saying her children were hungry. I wondered why. It was not the quality of the music I played. But my music, such as it was, did make me noticeable in a less strident way than calling out '¿una ayudita, por favor? Any spare change?' I was not an object of pity or resentment.

I also reflected on how I would fare with a different appearance. I was unwashed and my shirt was torn. But if you didn't look too closely, I dressed similarly to most men, and played what seemed to be an expensive musical instrument. I do not look Spanish and was clearly foreign. But I am fair-haired and blue-eyed, so I was a fellow European, a tourist. Respectable, familiar, acceptable. I imagined my experience, not only in Spain but across the western world, had I been the same person – a university-educated travel writer following the route of an old book that pleased me – but with dark skin or a keffiyeh.

What would the reaction have been, I wonder, had I looked like a Romanian gypsy or Moroccan immigrant, turning up in villages looking for somewhere to busk, a pavement to nap on and a nearby field to sleep in?

Camping

I ROUNDED A CORNER of the trail and a wide expanse of view fell away down a valley of oak trees. It was even more breathtaking for being unexpected. A broad blue river wound through the scene. I tore up my plans for a day of hefty mileage: I had to camp by that river. It was perfect. I had already busked, so I was carrying enough food.

Down on the riverbank, I dumped my sweaty pack and waded into the river. My feet sank in silky mud, soft as a cow's belly. I swam out carrying a bottle to fill with flowing water rather than dipping into the stagnant shallows. Then I lay on my back and drifted with the current, eyes closed, sunspots on my eyelids.

While I sat drying in the sun, the mud baking to dust on my feet, a speedboat roared upstream carrying three golden lads and girls, their tanned arms held aloft, hair blowing, big smiles. They did not notice me. I watched them bounce up the valley, the thrum of the engine already receding as their bow waves reached my riverbank. They were young and carefree and filled with summer, as Laurie will always be in my mind.

Revelling in the decadence of stopping early and bunking off work, I took time to choose a perfect patch of smooth ground to call home. Majestic old oaks framed the river view, their gnarled trunks carpeted with moss and branches fluffy with lichen. I swept aside acorns, shook out my sleeping bag and lit a small fire. I arranged my pan, food and diary within reach of where I sat. Back home, I am messy. Out on the road, perhaps yearning for home and structure, I am a methodical camper.

I chopped an onion and flung the skin into the river. A swirl of plump fish rose to investigate while I cooked. As I ate my rice, I wrote in my diary and smoke drifted across my face. Hills rose all around, forested up to the darkening sky. The evening stretched away, with sunset clouds floating westwards towards the sea where I began. A moth, yearning for the sun – greedy always for more, more, more – zithered round and round, ever closer to the fire until, in its frustrated madness, it plunged into the dazzling flame. I sipped hot water from my pan, pretended it was coffee and kept writing. My hips and shoulders ached, but this calm, wordless night of what the Japanese call *shinrin-yoku*, forest bathing, at least helped ease my mind.

When my travelling days are over, there will be a fond corner of my memory for all the nights I camped along the way: walking lightly upon the world, carrying all you need, pausing somewhere for rest and sanctuary. Nothing left behind but a crumpled patch of grass and the delicate tang of smoke tendrils. It is a satisfying way of life.

Well rested, I marched a comfortable 20 miles through woods and farmland. I stopped for the night on soft grass under rocky red hills. The skyline had a cleft at just the right position for the sunset. A river meander spilt over a natural weir into a sandy pool before narrowing and disappearing around the corner into reeds and trees. I wallowed in the shallows and washed my clothes. Under the water, the light was lime-clear and crisp as gin. Shoals of small sharp fish fled from my shadow. Bubbles fizzed and pebbles rattled beneath the weir. I held my breath, sank down and let the current push me across the pool and down the stream. Then I lay down to dry on a smooth boulder, my body shabby and sore, the sunshine and the breeze bathing me, refreshing, restoring.

When I woke in the moonless night it was so dark I could not even see my feet. But the stars a million miles away were shining, two thousand or more falling all the way down to the horizon. As my eyes adjusted, the layers of stars deepened as fainter ones came into focus. After appreciating the heavens for a few minutes, I was awake enough to bother to pee. So I knelt, shrugged my sleeping bag down to my waist, and peed from my sleeping mat. Proper en-suite luxury.

It was always a surprise and a pleasure to notice the Milky Way overhead, cleaving the sky in two. At home, I am disconnected from the wild world out there beyond the windows. I wish that gazing up at stars, not ceilings, was my nocturnal default. It is normal nowadays to spend most of our lives inside, temperature-controlled, light-switched, water-softened, air-freshened and double-glazed. We have become like babies in incubators, unable to survive in the world. I only sense the sterility of this when my situation is reversed and I spend so much time outside that going in feels strange once more. I am more at peace with myself and the world when I spend an extended period outdoors.

Changes

Human-powered journeys must be just that: an unbroken line made under your own steam. I have always been emphatic about this rule, no matter how difficult things become. No shortcuts, no bailing out, no hitching lifts. That is cheating. The tough times are the badge of honour you earn that sets you apart. I take a perverse pleasure in persevering though purgatory when everyone else would jack it in and call a taxi. I sneered at anyone who took more comfortable expedition options and envied those who suffered more than me. I regarded obduracy as a point of difference to be proud of.

But there were two different aspects to this journey:
1. The new skills I needed to learn.
2. How much of my established experience felt obsolete.

I was not enjoying myself today. I had ended up back on a busy road with traffic thundering by. The scenery was parched and drab. My feet hurt, my hips ached. Walking was tough. So I started to consider hitchhiking. And I did so precisely because for the past two decades I would have scorned the very suggestion.

The old *Adventure Al* would have insisted on walking every single step of the journey, regardless of whether parts of it were a waste of time. (In fact, he would have scoffed at this entire project. A few weeks walking in Spain? Call yourself an 'Adventurer'?)

The new *Adventure Al* still wanted to test himself, to attempt something hard and taste the spice of risk. But this time the challenge was not the physical beasting. It was not about being hard, wilfully suffering in order to overcome my weaker self and show the world how tough I was. My life had changed. I needed to change, too. This adventure was about vulnerability: my own, and those connected with playing the violin. There were miles to cover, but they did not really matter. I already knew I could walk a long way. I had done it many times before.

In truth, I was working on the new Al – the man – rather than the adventure stuff. Since settling down to family life I had lost my identity and washed up lonely and empty. The years I spent trying to outride and outsuffer everyone, charging madly at the world, were not a good model for the next 40 years.

My long bike ride came out of a longstanding fascination with world travel and endurance expeditions. During those years Lance Armstrong was one of my most significant role models. I cycled the world before he was outed as a cheating sociopath. It is hard to think of Lance now without the taint of drugs and bullying. But, back then, he ticked every box I wanted: the angry underdog crushing the competition through grit alone. I was young and wanted to stand apart from the world. When I was training to run the Marathon des Sables in the Sahara Desert, I tackled a marathon at home first, setting the target of beating Lance Armstrong's best time. That challenge drove me to finish in less than three hours, retching my guts out as I legged it past Big Ben in a race against the clock and Lance and myself. I pushed so hard that I had to walk downstairs backwards for a week.

'What am I on?' asked Lance in the Nike ad I watched a million times on YouTube before its deluded hubris became clear. 'I'm on my bike six hours a day busting my ass. What are you on?'

Then I failed to find a publisher for my book about cycling round the world. This is commonplace for unknown beginners. I kept writing anyway. As the rejections mounted I slogged away, hunched over a tiny desk beneath a poster of Lance. In my memory it rained every day I was writing that book, with rows of terraced houses lined up grey and drab outside the window. The poster showed Lance out on a training ride, alone, grinding up a mountain pass in the rain. The text below read, 'I rode, and I rode, and I rode. I rode like I had never ridden, punishing my body up and down every hill I could find . . . I rode when no one else would ride.' I decided to self-publish the book, to finish what I had started.

You can't cycle round the world. Who says I can't?

Your book is not good enough. Who says that?

This mindset got me up and over mountains and around the world. But since then things hadn't turned out too well for Lance, and they weren't great for me, either.

Who, then, did I want to become if I was no longer me or Lance? Being so tough on myself had to stop. Stop looking to prove myself, to impress people, to make a mark. I wanted to learn that it was acceptable to do something merely because it was enjoyable. I was trying to think differently, to become a new person. So I might as well try being somebody else. Laurie Lee seemed as good a person as any to pick.

Therefore, whenever I had a decision to make that summer, I did not ask my usual expedition questions: 'What's the toughest option? What will make the best story? What will people think?' Instead, I asked just one question: 'What would Laurie do?'

Vehicles thrashed by, one after the other. The noise and draught unnerved me. My eyes stung with fumes and dust and sweat. I asked myself what Laurie would have done if he was with me, walking along a busy road, hot and bothered, with all these comfortable options whizzing by?

Laurie once cadged a ride in a mule cart. The farmer talked about his work, glancing with disdain at Laurie's soft, work-shy English hands. 'It is different in some countries, I believe,' the farmer said, 'but God gave us a country we must fight like a lion.' He gave a loud cry and lashed the mules with his whip. On another occasion, Laurie 'was given a lift by two racy young booksellers' who 'pointed out all the brothels' along the way.

I stuck out my thumb.

Hitchhiking

I COULD NOT ENTIRELY cast aside my old habits and become an instant *flâneur*. I couldn't just sit on my rucksack and wait for someone to scoop me up and drive me to Madrid. So I continued walking, but with my thumb outstretched. My attitude, however, changed at once.

Until now I had accepted the day, albeit grumbling. I tolerated the heat and the noisy miles, and understood that I just needed to grind down this road for a few hours before I got back to my quiet paths and forests. But once escape became an option I could think of nothing else. I fantasised about air-conditioning, music, speed. I pleaded with every car that passed.

'Please stop. Please, please, please!' I smiled, trying to make eye contact with the drivers and appear friendly. 'You look nice and kind.'

'*¡Vete a la mierda, cabrón!*' I swore every time a vehicle drove by without stopping. 'Screw you!'

Those selfish, lazy people! How dare they not snap out of their conversations, slam on the brakes in the middle of their busy day and go out of their way to help a bloke who looked like a tramp? I sulked down the road as car after car roared past.

At last! A car pulled up. Selfish sod turned benevolent saviour in an instant. Hazard lights blinked and I whooped at the thrill of surprise and uncertainty. Hitchhiking is an invitation to be a guest in someone else's story for a time. It is a beguiling prospect when you've spent too long immersed in your own solo show. I jogged to the driver's window as quickly as I was able with my rucksack.

'*¡Muchas gracias!*' I gushed, trying to look friendly and unthreatening.

The driver smiled and climbed out to open the boot. We shook hands and introduced ourselves, the instant gut judgements of two people choosing to trust one another. Miguel wore an ironed shirt and his aftershave smelled good. Expensive sunglasses perched on his head. He helped me lower my heavy bag into his car.

'Careful with the violin, *cuidado con el violín,*' I cautioned, by which I really meant, 'Look! I've got a violin. I'm interesting and safe. Let's go! *¡Vámonos!*'

I piled into the car, filled with family but just enough room for me. Mum in the front urged her two boys to shuffle up and make space on the back seat. She did not speak again. I sensed that stopping for me had not been her suggestion. Doors slammed. The noise, the fumes, the heat and glare vanished. In their place: air-conditioning and music! The kids, squeezed in beside me, stared. I did my best not to smell, a tricky task in a small car. Miguel slid his seat forwards to give me a little more leg room. Then came that anticipated press on the accelerator pedal and suddenly I was barrelling eastwards, cheating happily as the world raced by at warp speed. Good idea, Laurie!

We began the traditional question-and-answer routine of hitchhiking strangers. My destination and theirs, where I was from, all our names. Miguel talked to me via the rear-view mirror. They were going to a river for a picnic.

'A perfect family day: my favourite thing,' declared Miguel with a smile, before enquiring about my life back home.

'Yes, I have children,' I told him. 'A boy and a girl, about the same age as your lads. I miss them.'

I fell quiet at this, and Miguel changed the subject. He asked about the violin, assuming I was a musician.

'Definitely not!' I laughed. 'But I dared myself to pretend that I was.'

Even his wife was amused as I explained my trip. The idea of living without money and facing public shame struck a chord with Miguel.

'*Eres valiente.*'

I demurred, but the flattery was as welcome as the music and soft seats.

'I could never go away on a journey like yours,' he added, after a moment's reflection.

I basked again in my bravery.

'I would miss my family too much to leave them for as long as you have done.'

I smiled wryly at my mistake.

We had already driven four kilometres, barely enough time for one song on the radio. But they were turning here, so I had to get out. Miguel apologised, but there was no need. Kind acts are amplified when you are alone and abroad, and he had given me more than just a cheated couple of miles.

'Here we are. Good luck!'

That hitchhike was a deliberate sabotage of my walk and my old principles. It forced me to relax and become less puritanical. It also brought more human connection into the trip. I enjoyed it and so hitched a few more rides in the coming weeks when I was bored, impatient or suffering.

My next ride was with a young man in a BMW on his way to the doctor. David was worried about his appointment but he didn't want to talk about it. Was he hoping for a dash of good karma by picking me up? Probably he just wanted to take his mind off things.

David's friends had all moved to the cities for work, but he had chosen to remain in his home village. He operated diggers for construction companies and enjoyed a low-stress, non-materialistic life. When I teased him gently about having a BMW, David bristled, missing my jokey tone. He explained at length that the car was old, he had bought it cheap and it would last a long time. He drove fast, chewing a toothpick, and beat a rhythm with his fingers on the steering wheel.

'I like what you are doing,' said David. 'Your whole life on your back. Just the stuff you need and a bit of money. Maybe I will be able to do it, one day. We'll see.'

I watched the white lines zip by in the reflection of his sunglasses.

You can never anticipate the direction conversations may take in the confessional intimacy of hitchhiking. A man stopped his moped alongside me – straw hat, open shirt, crucifix, big belly. He couldn't give me a lift, he apologised, with beer on his breath, but he wanted to be useful. I had not asked for help and was in no hurry. I was happy walking. But he stood in the middle of the gravel road anyway, flicked away his cigarette, flagged down the next vehicle and commandeered it for me. I was being forced to hitchhike, and I was too amused to refuse.

I climbed up into the van, driven by a farmhand in a sleeveless blue boiler suit. He was a little older than me and happy to give me a ride. We talked as we bounced along the farm track, swerving potholes, dust swirling through the open windows. Iago had a ready smile and lots to say. He had twice walked the Camino de Santiago, Spain's famous pilgrimage trail, which lay close to the route I was walking. Picking me up brought back memories of those days.

'I wish I could do it again. But those times are past. I won't have the chance again.'

Iago had walked the Camino with his wife; the first time to enjoy an adventure together, the second to fulfil a promise to a dying friend. They had been the best days of his life, he recalled, just him and his wife out there together in the hills.

'You should do it again,' I said. 'It would be special.'

'We got divorced last month.'

The sudden smallness of the silent vehicle swallowed me.

Loneliness

IN MANY WAYS I feel the sharp end of solitude more when I'm back from the wild. At home, I am a lonely writer. I work in a shed that measures five leisurely paces across, or four purposeful ones. It is my oasis and teleporter. There are pictures on the walls of rivers, mountains, stars, the sea. Stained glass on one window catches the early sunlight; it shows the waterfall where we used to swim in my Yorkshire childhood. I have pinned a big world map to the ceiling, alongside the *Born to Run* LP sleeve and photographs of the *James Caird* and Scott at the South Pole. Ordnance Survey maps paper one wall and all the bookshelves. I have a globe, a Red Ensign I picked up when running on a North Sea beach, and number plates from Iceland and Arabia. There are rows of travel books, the dregs of a whisky bottle or two, a pile of old *National Geographic*s and an untidy overspill of books on the floor, among rugs from Iraq and Afghanistan. On my desk is a framed relief map of Suilven – my favourite mountain – a few conkers, a pendant of turned cedar from Paris, driftwood from Canada and the Caribbean, stones picked up on my travels and a 90-year-old penny I found in a local stream.

I pass most of my working days in this shed, drinking tea and listening to the radio. It is where I am writing these words. I spend a lot of time by myself and am often lonely. I have no local social life. I don't drop into the pub or have any training buddies. I don't have friends who pop round un-announced to talk of mad ideas or lend me a book.

When I plan journeys, it is the prospect of empty landscapes that appeals most. Yet when I return from an adventure, it is the human interactions that linger in the memory. I relished the isolation of crossing Iceland but preferred how much my friend and I laughed together out there. I walked solo through India but was never far from a friendly cup of chai and a chat about cricket. Rowing the Atlantic with three companions, inching across a month-and-a-half of emptiness, forged friends for life.

Since arriving in Spain, conversations had flavoured every day. Fragments of interaction, a few words, even a smile: this walk was more sociable than anything else I have done. Its success depended on my engaging with people and getting a response to my music. I needed to trust the goodwill of entire towns without knowing anyone there.

Chance meetings are one of the great joys of travel. From my experience around the world, I was confident that nearly everyone I encountered would be kind. In addition, under-taking something unusual and challenging made it more likely that people would respond with enthusiasm. This trust freed me to head into the unknown – as Laurie put it – 'still soft at the edges, but with a confident belief in good fortune'.

The People of this Earth

My musical repertoire was a handful of brief songs, chosen by Becks for their simplicity, and played poorly. But they were my only weapons, my totems, and we travelled together across the summer. These tunes became the soundtrack to all the occasions I failed to earn money or the sparkling instances of success. I even hummed them as I walked through the fields between villages. The music was the link between all the people I met in the villages I walked through.

> *Yo soy un hombre sincero,*
> *De donde crece la palma,*
> *Y antes de morir yo quiero*
> *Echar mis versos del alma.*

> I am an honest man,
> From the place where the palm tree grows.
> And before I die I want to
> Sing out the verses of my soul.

A bald pensioner in a snazzy purple shirt. Twenty cents bagged within the first 20 minutes of playing! The thrill and relief of earning the first coin never diminished. That coin was key, I learned. It gave me belief: this was possible. I can do this, I have not failed, I will eat today. The success made me puff out my chest and play with more conviction. This often generated more interest. No wonder a mere *gracias* sounded insufficient. The gentleman carried on his way, waving away my thanks.

A Basque family on holiday and in relaxed mood. I reminisced with them about a night I once spent in their town, San Sebastián, sleeping on a diving platform out in the bay to save money on a hotel. Three of us bundled our clothes into bin bags and swam out to the platform. We were delighted with our accommodation: it had the best view in town of the curved beach and forested hills. But it began to rain hard in the night and we shivered until dawn. The family laughed exclaiming, 'you should have stayed with us!' The dad and his toddler tried my violin, passing the time until their restaurant reservation was ready. They gave 50 cents.

A dark-haired man. About my age, observing from behind his sunglasses and grinning. He knew I was terrible. But he also knew that I knew that. He loitered, intrigued, on the fringes of my vision. I sensed he might flee if I pressed him, so I said *hola*, gave what I hoped was a knowing smile and kept playing, and waiting. Make your cast, reel in the line. Play your song, see who bites. Eventually, curiosity overcame shyness and he walked over to chat when I changed my music sheets. He laughed at what I was trying to do, and handed me a euro.

The guests of a wedding party. The lads all puffed chests and swagger and boozy banter. The young women tottering behind in high heels, clutching their skirts and each other. Two flower girls in pretty white dresses, absorbed by their messy chocolate ice creams. The boisterous blokes, amused by my playing, emptied their pockets in a rambunctious splurge of loose coins, some of which landed in the violin case. I bought a packet of half-price Frosties to celebrate, and my teeth dissolved with happiness. 'It seems that I'd come to the right country,' noted Laurie. 'Poor as it was, the pennies were few, but they were generously given.'

My first donation from a teenager, wearing a vest and a backwards baseball cap. He gave all of five cents, though he did it with sincerity. Another boy peered into my case. One meagre coin. He was not impressed. I told him to return later and look again, for this night was going to make me rich. I was confident! He did return later, and there were indeed a few more coins. He looked impressed. Or at least he looked surprised, which is not quite the same thing.

A Bob Geldof lookalike, approaching at speed. Waving a banknote in the air and smiling as though he knew me, as though he had come out just to give me money. Neither was true. I was dumbfounded. Both he and his wife smiled and radiated goodwill. I explained the impact that five euros would have for me compared to someone less cash-strapped. I asked if I could take a photograph with them, but they declined, wished me well and walked away with a wave.

A 5-year-old girl appearing from nowhere in a light blue dress. She grabbed my violin by the neck as I was packing away the music stand and lifted it above her head. I froze. I didn't want to scare her into dropping it. Her dad did the same, aghast. He saw a Stradivarius; I saw my summer's meal tickets. It was a surreally long instant. All those hard miles, all the months practising in my shed, everything compressed now to the whim of a little girl with a ponytail. Then her big sister walked up, unaware of the fizzing panic. She placed a coin in my violin case and turned away, pricking the tension as the girl spotted her, put the violin down gently and trotted along behind. Her dad and I exhaled.

An elegant lady with white hair and pearl earrings. She presented 50 cents with a nod and a straight back before I had even played a note. Later, my busking over, I listened to a folk concert in the plaza. The same lady caught my eye and beckoned me to her café table. Dancers filled the stage, twirling in long, bright skirts to the music of oboes, castanets and guitars. I greeted the lady and her husband, then crouched beside her in a cloud of perfume. She apologised to me, hoping it had not offended my artistic sensibilities that she had deigned to tip me before I even began to play. My music case was empty and she had donated out of pity. I reassured her that everyone did that. She laughed and patted my arm. Pity paid. Laurie knew this, too, though he had far more skill than me. 'To arouse pity or guilt was always good for a penny, but that was as far as it got you; while a tuneful appeal to the ear, played with sober zest, might often be rewarded with silver.'

I watched the folk festival for a while, but what I really wanted to do was lie down in a quiet field and fall asleep. So that is what I did. One indulgence of travelling solo is doing whatever the hell you want, whenever you want. The downside is being occasionally forlorn among laughing friends and lovers with entwined hands. Laurie talked about wandering 'invisibly among them, submerged by their self-absorption; and suddenly found myself wishing for a face I knew, for Stroud on a Saturday night . . .'

Siesta

THAT SUMMER I WALKED hundreds of miles of green lanes and limestone heights, through wheat fields brown and crisp as parchment paper. The one factor common to every landscape, spread across the sky and crushing the land beneath it, was the sun. Englishmen and midday sun do not mix. The fierceness of Spain's high summer ground me down.

In towns the sun oppressed with the relentless heat of the streets. Hot car roofs, restaurant extractor fans, radiating tarmac, pungent dog shit: heat comes at you from all angles. Out in the countryside the heat simply head-punches from above. It is dry and emotionless, pushing down on you like a car crusher. I am fine, I am fine, and then I buckle, collapsing into the next patch of shade, dreaming of the heights ahead, anticipating springs and cool pine forests.

Early in the trip I tried to absorb the heat and beat it, walking myself into stubborn delirium. But the sun always won. It crumpled me and consumed me, forcing me to flee. 'Throughout the afternoon,' Laurie wrote, 'I drowsed behind the café curtains, hiding from the worst of the heat. The streets were empty now except for a few thin dogs hugging the walls for an inch of shade. All else was silence, blinding white, while the sun moved higher over the town.'

I once found the ideal siesta spot on a riverbank shaded by willow trees. The current had created a soft grey beach on the inside curve. Upstream stood a dozen spans of Roman bridge, fish rising in the pool above, burbling rapids below. Two fishermen on the bridge considered their options, the latest generation in centuries of optimists. Downstream, tangled piles of bleached logs showed the river's winter power. Today, though, the water was clear green and calm. I swam. My legs looked skinny.

I crunched a carrot for lunch and studied a dead pike on the bank, as long as my leg and staring blankly back at me. Flies nibbled its eye. Laurie trumped my carrot, whiling away his siesta on this same river with a bottle of wine and a bag of plums. Black cormorants, clustered, flew upstream at speed. I dived back into the river.

Another day I found shade under the arches of a police station. A tramp snored a few metres away. I kept an eye on the time from his watch, which was useful, if unexpected, for I didn't have one myself. His straw hat had slipped to the ground and his dirty fingers curved protectively around the frame of an old bike. The police tolerated the pair of us for a couple of hours until a cop nudged me with his boot and grunted that it was time to move on.

'Please can I stay just a bit longer?' I pleaded. 'Until it is less hot? Then I promise I'll leave and never come back.'

The policeman relented and ducked back inside to his air-conditioning. The tramp nodded his thanks to me. We then fell back to sleep. I dozed with my head pillowed on my rucksack, my eyes shaded beneath my hat. Siestas in public places are a series of plummeting into and ejecting out of snatches of deep sleep as cars rev or dustbins clang or policemen plod. When the temperature dropped below my rising impatience, I staggered, bleary, back out into the heat.

I mastered the art of picking prime siesta spots. Dead ends and alleyways were good, as I was more likely to be left alone. That was worth the occasional whiff of stale urine. A concave corner of wall, facing northeast, gave shade for the longest time. Elsewhere, you had to keep moving, chasing the compass to hide from the sun.

One siesta I shuffled after shadows for hours, beginning on a bench in a triangular plaza, my toes tickled by geraniums. The plaza was little more than a meeting of three lanes. Flat on my back, I watched two butterflies cavort like Morse code across the empty blue, backlit and beautiful. Grass seeds drifted like white asterisks. Eagles glided overhead; migrating cranes flew higher still. I saw one or two planes, the first in weeks. Even the sky was quiet here. Contrails formed, chalk slashes, then billowed to nothing in the dry air.

I was replete with happiness, at peace, not wanting to change a thing. I try to take notice of these times when I am happy, for they are rarer than I might like. They are precious and too easy to overlook. A woman walked by carrying a tray of eggs. She was the only other person outdoors in this midday heat. She had moved to this village from Barcelona.

'I love my Sierra,' she told me. 'And now these mountains are my home.'

'I wish I lived among mountains,' I replied. And so ended my in-the-moment happiness! When she left, her perfume lingered, along with the isolation of knowing she was making an effort for someone else, while nobody knew or cared that I was here.

When my bench ran out of shade I moved from the geraniums to the pavement outside a house. I sewed up a tear in my shirt and hung my sleeping bag up to air. It was a beautiful village of narrow cobbled pathways and old cottages. I was fast asleep when a woman stepped out of her house and almost tripped over me. She was unperturbed to find a sweaty Englishman lying on her doorstep. She offered me a glass of cold water and then brought a chair for me to sit on. That is always one of my favourite luxuries when living an outdoor life.

Daily Bread

MY WALK REMAINED FRAGILE, and the line between success and panic was faint. I cheered in delight, for example, the morning I found a 20-cent coin on the street. But often I walked into villages and my heart sank at their smallness. They might be nothing more than a crossroads with a cluster of buildings and a bus stop, a new commuter community with no shops or infrastructure, or so small that I could already see the fields on the other side. Other times the village was big enough but I arrived at the wrong time of day, when everybody was indoors and there were more pigeons than people. There were very few hours of daylight when you could expect to find people out and about. I just kept walking straight through all these villages, reducing rations and increasing mileage until I found a place to play.

The challenge of busking from village to village in Spain has become harder in the three generations since Laurie walked here. When he entered villages, 'black-robed women, standing in doorways, made soft exclamations' as he passed. 'Children ran from the alleys and encircled me and ushered me noisily into the village. "Look at the foreigner!" they cried, as though they had made me up. "Look at the *rubio* who's come.'"

But today a stillness lay over Spain. There was a noticeable lack of bustle. Walking in Spain was the opposite of walking through India, where the villages were alive with children walking to school in clean white shirts, hawkers pushing wooden trolleys and women chatting as they pumped water into battered metal pots. Every moment busy and lived outdoors. But everything had gone from this corner of Spain with the recession – the work, the people, the soul – gone to Madrid or Miami. There was little reason to remain, no future here. Villages had become retirement homes.

I rested in a bus shelter outside a row of shuttered homes, another disappointing busking prospect. I was fed up. Sweating midday hours in scraps of shade is perhaps the most enduring constant of my adventuring life. Stapled to the walls were posters for saint day carnivals, flyers for bus tours to Disneyland Paris and an advert for a flat to rent, complete with little tear-off strips of phone numbers. Nobody had torn off a number so I took one, thinking it might give a small boost of hope to the landlord. Obsessed with food, I popped the paper into my mouth and began to chew. Then, realising that I had been reduced subconsciously to eating paper, I spat the pulp onto the road.

I lay down on the dirty floor, shirt off, socks off, too heat-struck to bother unfolding my sleeping mat or bundle my shirt into a pillow. Occasionally in those bus shelters a breath of breeze washes coolness across your sweaty chest. But not that day. The only solace was luxuriating in the pain pulsing up my legs from my feet and knowing that this was a pleasure compared to walking with a heavy pack on a hard road.

*   *   *

I heard a car slow, then park. The door slammed. I peered out from beneath my hat. A pair of trousers, bags of shopping, a loaf of bread tucked under an arm. I tugged on my shirt and limped into the sunlight to ask where the nearest shop was.

'*Está lejos,*' the man told me. 'It's a long way. Too far to walk.'

He turned towards his home and lunch. Then he paused, put down his bags, tore the loaf and offered me half. I protested. But he just shrugged. Take, eat, he said. No big deal. And he walked away without another word. Spontaneous kindness with a shrug and without a second thought: the best type of all. Back in my bus shelter, I smiled, plucking at the soft centre of the warm wheat loaf of *pan de cea*.

The Music in Me

WHEN I WALK I sing old songs to remind me of old times. I travel for new experiences, yet wherever I go I carry the memories that originally drove me away, as well as the multitudes of joy and wonder of all the places I've been.

I begin every adventure with Willie Nelson's celebration of being 'On the Road Again'. I sing it on the first morning and at all the new beginnings after that. When I cycled round the world there were many of these. I was by myself for weeks at a time, riding from one country to the next. I would pause in cities to rest, obtain visas, give talks at schools, or repair my bike. Human connections, relationships and friendships rushed to fill the vacuum. But before I knew it, it was time to leave again.

Those four years sometimes felt reduced to a cycle of saying hello, waving goodbye. So many departures ground me down. Occasionally I lost my nerve and conjured excuses to stay a little longer, craving stillness and community. I would delay for a few days until I mustered the bravery to pack my panniers once again – two bags on the front of the bike, two on the back, strap my tent on top and go. Everything in its place, an illusion of order and constancy – home, perhaps – amid the flux and rootlessness of a nomadic bike ride.

Then I waved goodbye and cycled away once more into the spaces of the landscape and my thoughts. Arriving as a stranger, becoming friends, leaving forever. Crowded cities, empty tent. A lonely sadness until the frisson of anonymous freedom bounced back, the thrill of limitless potential that is the enormity of the world and the fuel of all long journeys.

I let my subconscious pick the songs, skipping those which added to maudlin mindsets. I rarely needed help spiralling downwards into sadness. But the right song could shake me up and get me whistling, like Bob Dylan's 'Song to Woody'. 'I'm thousands of miles from my home,' I sang, out there on another continent, walkin' a road through Tamil Nadu's warm dawn, the day about to be born, low-slung and steeped with the smells of cooking fires and kerosene. White egrets scratched for insects among gleaming green banana fronds as I munched a pocketful of biscuits, my legs eager for miles. Nothing beats the optimism of a morning good mood on a journey.

Remembering breaking trail in Greenland now, Tom Waits and me, a song called 'Hold On', and the snow crunching beneath my skis. 'You've got to hold on, Al. Just hold on.' The starkness of a world reduced to white beneath a blank blue sky. The ice ocean-flat all the way to the mountainous horizon. I held course by a compass mounted to a chest harness. My frozen eyelashes felt heavy as I blinked, and the sledge dragged behind me like an anchor. I was breathing hard but I needed to concentrate. I did not want to let anybody down.

Life on a three-man expedition can be more isolated than travelling alone. You ski in single file, taking turns each session to break trail or follow the man in front, pacing yourself to save energy but knowing you need to be fast. The muffling effect of thick clothing, skis scouring the ice and strong wind makes conversation impossible. Your buddies so close, yet you march inside your own world. Just you, your thoughts and sometimes your music. After 90 minutes you all come together for a 10-minute break. Eat. Pee. Share an idea. Go again.

I was filled with a deep well of joy and an appreciation of my good fortune to be out on that isolated ice cap. The magnitude, the beauty, the skills for self-sufficiency. But a knot of guilt soured the joy. The price of my fulfilment was the burden of childcare and exhaustion doubling on Sarah back home. I felt additional remorse from the relief coursing through me at being away from all that. Remote Greenland, cold and strewn with crevasses, was easier to navigate than life at home. And I knew that this expedition was merely training for the next one. That would always be the case.

My goggles misted with tears as I lamented how my happiness made my family sad. I was trying to live in two incompatible worlds. My legs were tired, but I must not slow my pace. Don't let anyone down. My stomach growled, and Tom Waits growled at me to hold on, hold on, hold on . . .

This was all so far from the distant, unshackled days as a young man when my only baggage was what I could carry and the songs and dreams in my heart. Lead-grey water, solid and marbled, thundered upon the yacht. The wind still rising, 50 knots now. The folly of a small boat in a big ocean, foaming fury, wind howling in the rigging. I clawed my way, hand over hand, careful as hell, up to the bow to pack down the last scrap of sail. I would not have guessed that one day I would choose to return to these waves in a rowing boat.

I yelled out my favourite Foo Fighters song in triumph and fear with the yacht heeling hard and the salt spray stinging. It's times like these when you truly learn to live. Music to make me strong. Adventures to feel alive and remarkable where those unaccustomed would experience only terror. Can I handle it, or should I run away and leave all this behind? Chasing the four winds of the earth to make myself feel worthy. The wind snatched my words and flung them into the angry sky.

Such is the power of music that, plodding through Spain on the cusp of my fortieth birthday, my mind could leap from that reckless, youthful adventure in a Tehuantepec storm to something I could never have imagined back then: dancing around my kitchen (having a kitchen, a home!), with my daughter (a daughter! *My* daughter!). The radio volume turned up to 11, and Lucy's tiny hands wrapped in mine as we spun together. The song itself did not matter, but the moment did, and I never wanted to forget 'And a Bang on the Ear' for the fullness of this feeling. I lifted my girl above my head, and our eyes met, filled with laughter and love.

We have no say in what becomes the soundtrack to our years, the songs that accompany the screenplay of stories and characters unfurling before us. The road is signposted with musical surprises. Songs show up, happen, hang around and become your life.

Hurrying to the hospital before my first child was born,

the moon looming in the night sky. Sarah was already there, ready. The nurses had booted me out of the ward at nightfall. The phone jolted me awake, alone in our bed at home.

'It's time.'

I drove fast through the darkness, cautioning myself not to crash, not to die, my senses all on fire. I turned on the radio. Out of the lottery of random radio lyrics, Newton Faulkner was not too bad, crooning that if he could have only one night, then he would choose 'right now'.

That was the song, that was the night, and tears streamed down my face. I was saying goodbye to my solitary life where it was up to me if I drove fast, gambled with my life, lived on the edge. I was racing to welcome my son into the world. It was about us now. The greatest adventure about to begin.

Jungle

I CLIMBED AN OVERGROWN footpath to a pass, breathing hard. Up there I stumbled upon a perfect blue rectangle: a swimming pool, incongruous in the woods and hills. It belonged to a village hidden beyond the next rise. Today, however, the pool was deserted, and I was lost. I had only Laurie for company. 'I followed the track through the hills, but saw only occasional signs of life . . . The track climbed higher into the clear cold air, and I just followed it, hoping to keep direction.'

I had been following forestry paths that kept zigging when I wanted them to zag. So I left the path and turned instead along a cutting, beneath a fizzing power line slung between giant pylons. This route worked for a while, but I lost my nerve as the cable drifted away from the direction I needed to go, contouring round a deep valley. If I followed it, I would be committed to the route for the rest of the day, wherever it took me.

I changed tack again and headed straight down the hillside, cross country. I saw a quarry far below, the machinery tiny as Lego. Its access road would be an escape route if I could somehow get down to it. But the descent turned into a mini-epic. I plummeted down the slope through head-high bracken that tugged and clutched at me. I struggled, pushing forwards, unable to see where I was going. The bracken held me upright as I half swam, half tumbled down the mountain.

It became difficult to make progress. The hillside was as tangled as a jungle. There was no chance of forcing my way back up again. I was committed. I shouted at the sky, frustrated but amused, and ploughed on. As I struggled I felt once more the animal joy of being alive that used to course through me so often. I kept on wriggling downwards. Drop anything, and it would be lost. Drop dead, and nobody could find my body. The undergrowth enveloped me. It was exhausting, but fun in a way. This was, after all, the closest I had got to a hug all summer.

I eventually reached the valley floor but now found myself at the top of a 12-foot retaining wall. I scrambled down it into the quarry, out of breath, scratched, cross, and grinning. I was saved! By now it was dusk and I was shattered. I unrolled my sleeping bag beside a tractor. It was an uncomfortable night, but weary relief sent me to sleep. 'When twilight came, I curled up where I was, too exhausted to mind the cold.'

Postman

BY THE TIME I reached a village, I was sunbaked and disgruntled, craving cold Coke and ice cream, but unable to afford either. There were few people around, so it was once again pointless to busk. I was tempted to stop for a siesta, but it was too early. I tried to dredge up the resolve to keep walking. I asked an old lady in her garden how far it was to the next town. About 15 kilometres, she thought. I groaned. The heat would be brutal before I arrived.

Seeing that her answer had deflated me, the lady checked with the postman who was just handing her a letter. He agreed with her estimate, but he also offered me a lift, so long as I didn't mind delivering letters along the way. He said he would enjoy the company. I laughed and shook his hand. At home, when I catch myself getting more stressed about work than I ever intended to be, I dream of becoming a postman in the Shetland Isles. I told Marcelino about my postman fantasy as we climbed into his car.

'It's hard work and bad money.' He turned the key and dismissed my career-change thoughts. 'Things used to be much better.'

We drove out of the village onto expanses of open heath.

'This whole area used to be wheat,' Marcelino explained, sweeping his arm. The farmers abandoned it because the grain price fell so low. A few fallow years would be good for the earth, though the local economy was suffering in the meantime.

Marcelino had been a postman for three decades. Every day he drove the same 140-kilometre circuit round 15 villages. He was now looking forward to retirement. In each village we parked the car then walked around delivering the letters. There were not many, mostly junk mail or bank statements. We had to collect the mail, too, though every post box was empty. Amazon had made most postmen busier these days, said Marcelino, but not his communities filled with old people.

Marcelino was placid but brisk, stooped but with a swift, bird-like stride. He did not rush, but nor did he waste a moment. Every movement was efficient. I scurried alongside him, a head taller, sore hips rolling my gait. Freed of the weight of my rucksack, I felt I was walking on air. Marcelino greeted everyone by name. A few of them laughed and enquired about his dusty 'helper'.

The villages we visited were Spain's usual mix of handsome traditional homes, dilapidated old ones and ugly, cheap new builds. Lots of houses had bottles filled with water on their steps. Marcelino said it was to stop stray dogs peeing on them, but I couldn't tell if he was being serious. The old farmhouses hid behind high walls with imposing doors, tall and broad enough for loaded carts to have passed through. The doors were made from stout boards of oak studded with rivets and large keyholes.

Eighty years ago, Laurie often slept in the courtyards behind these doors. I was disappointed never to get invited inside one, where Laurie 'found the usual spacious barn hanging with freshly watered flowers. A few low chairs stood around the walls, and there was a table and tiled stove in the corner. All was cool and bare. Chickens pecked at the floor and swallows flashed from the high arched ceiling.'

At noon, as the church bell chimed, we stopped for *café con leche*. It was Marcelino's daily ritual, punctual and precise. Stepping indoors during the Spanish summer offers a similar relief to diving into a pool. My eyes took time to adjust. Two builders sat at the bar, tape measures and pencils poking from back pockets beneath broad shoulders. One was drinking beer, the other liquor. One was bald under his cap, the other had thick black hair and was thumbing through Facebook on his phone. They were the only customers. Nobody spoke.

An old man followed us into the café, knocked back a shot of *aguardiente*, slid a coin across the bar, then walked back home for lunch. He did not remove his straw hat or say a word. He came every day, Marcelino told me.

A clip frame on the wall held photos of the annual village feast. The photos were amateur, with people squinting or looking the wrong way: normal snapshots of everyday life in an ordinary village. I found them fascinating, though, because it was new to me. Each summer the community came together to roast a pig, Marcelino explained, a big one weighing around 200 kilograms. He stretched his arms wide and grinned. Men burned off the pig's skin and hair on a straw bonfire, then grilled the meat while women prepared long tables in the plaza. The entire village sat down together to a feast of ham and eggs. And then, at midnight, the dancing began.

The waitress carried the coffees to our table. I reached into my pocket to pay, but Marcelino waved me away.

'You are my guest.'

His generosity was fortunate because I remembered then
that I had no money. I could not have paid. The restriction
was wearing. I disliked being unable to repay someone's kindness. It reminded me to be grateful that at home I did have
money, and the easy freedom and little daily luxuries that
grants me. Only when something is taken away do I learn to
appreciate it.

Waving goodbye to Marcelino, I made my way through expansive irrigated fields. White storks foraged for grubs among
the crops. The farms were more extensive and efficient here
than the quaint, photogenic, struggling ones back in Galicia.
When Laurie walked this region, the earth was arid 'with its
fields of copper earth, its violent outcrops of poppies running
in bloodstained bandanas across acres of rasping wheat'. Today,
the miles of maize, cabbages, lettuces and tomatoes reminded
me of walking down supermarket aisles. I pinched a carrot
from a field. I was proud not to have needed to resort to this
regularly, but I did enjoy crunching it as I walked. The rotating
arms of irrigation sprayers spluttered by, and I had to time
each passing to dodge a soaking. Concrete channels carried
river water from upstream, brimful and burbling. I cupped my
hands and drank, too thirsty to worry about pesticides and
stomach upset.

Amid miles of cabbages – the horizon low, the sky high – I
stripped for an impromptu cold shower, naked in the whirling
sprayers. Refreshment for the body, amusement for the mind.
Both are valuable on long, hard days.

The Greatest Day

DAWN BROKE ON THE greatest day of them all, slowly
and quietly like every other day. I approached a town perched
on a hill like a fairy tale. At the top stood a squat castle with
cylindrical corner towers. I crossed a medieval stone bridge
and wound up a cobbled road, pushing with my hiking poles
to help me up the gradient. I rested at the castle walls and
looked down at the river below, wide and inviting for swimming.

Loud rock music jarred with the pastoral view. It was
accompanying a mountain bike race that culminated in a cruel,
out-of-the-saddle climb to the castle. Two riders raced each
other, hell for leather, elbow to elbow, matching each pedal
stroke, pain versus pride. The winners had long since finished.
This was personal. Their lungs rasped, their muddy faces
creased with agony. I joined the crowd cheering them on. Just
before the finish both men reached out a hand and called it a
draw. They freewheeled laughing across the line, holding
hands. The announcer on the PA system praised their *espíritu*
and cranked up the music.

I scrounged a slice of watermelon from the finishers' table in the shade of the castle. I slurped the fruit and cheered the stragglers. My mood lifted with the music and the lively weekend atmosphere. Then I walked down the hill to scope out a busking spot, optimistic now about my chances.

The street corner I found was not ideal, with only a moderate flow of pedestrians. I stacked my kit beside a cash machine and prepared to play. The wedge of shade was small so I would soon face the full force of the sun. A row of parked cars blocked my view, and there were spatterings of sheep shit everywhere from a flock led through town en route to higher grazing pastures. But despite this, I received my first donation within minutes. And this day they just kept on coming.

By the time the shade had expired and the town lulled towards siesta, I had earned 20 euros and 5 cents, plus two ice-cold Cokes from a tour group waiting for their coach! No man needs such wealth. It was wonderfully, hilariously ludicrous. I pressed the cool can to my head and burped loudly.

I was filled with the delight that comes when you put yourself out there, give it a go, and all your stars align. Days you remember all your life. The half-volley strike that flies straight and true. The sunset wave that rises, turquoise and gold, lifting your board and hurtling you to glory. That day on your travels when the sun was warm on the cobbles and your pockets were full of silver, and everything was just the way you had always hoped it might be once again.

I blew two decadent euros on an ice cream, a classic chocolate Magnum that tasted all the better for being a treat. It lasted about 10 seconds. Then I bought bread, chorizo, tomatoes, tuna and peanuts, and celebrated with a tomato sandwich. I allowed myself to feel proud about the day. On expeditions, I have always berated myself for being weak, making mistakes or performing badly. It was time I learned also to say 'well done'.

Evening

EVENING MILES WERE A mix of weariness and satisfaction. I was impatient for the day to be over, to ease the pain in my shoulders and feet, to eat and to sleep. My pack was heavy, as I always carried extra water for the night. But it was a time of contentment, too. The heat's fury gone, replaced by a weary sense of accomplishment and a mounting curiosity about where I might lay my head.

As I packed away my violin and prepared to begin my evening miles, a woman in a white dress gave me a peach. Soft, pink, smooth and beautiful. I caressed the peach as I walked, squeezed it, smelled it, savoured it for as long as I could resist. Then I bit into the sweet, juicy flesh. It was exquisite! I have never enjoyed fruit so much. I promised myself that, when I had money again, I would eat a peach every single day, knowing even as I said it that I would not.

I followed winding *cañadas*, the ancient droving roads, through open fields. An old shepherd mumbled to his sheep as he plodded wearily homeward, dust rising from the flock and glowing in the light. The same scene has happened daily for hundreds, maybe thousands of years. At the end of a narrow footpath, halfway up a hill of shorn blond wheat, stood the ruins of a chapel. The roof had long since fallen, and a sycamore had taken root in the sacristy. Its tall trunk rose from the rubble and the canopy crowned the small building. As I approached, a shower of white doves burst from the chapel. After a moment of confusion they drew together in a flock then flew north. I paused by the tree, leaning against the crumbling wall to rest. I watched the birds in the clear sky. They flew with such purpose. I wondered if they knew where they were going, or if it was just ingrained in them to go. They would return later to roost in this sycamore after I had gone, circling before settling soft as snow in the branches.

Dotted across the undulating landscape were stone barns and houses with broad lintels and solid doors that reminded me of the Yorkshire Dales where I grew up. Many were abandoned. I fantasised about renovating a home here and I whiled away a few miles with unrealistic daydreams of a new life in Spain. I remembered the simpler years when moving to a hilltop village would have been as straightforward as deciding to do so, and making it happen.

I greeted a group of old ladies as I passed through their village, tucked in a cleft of hills. They were sitting outside their homes in the mellow sunshine, arms folded, watching their day draw to a close. One pointed at my laden rucksack with her walking stick and warned, 'Don't sleep outside around here, *jóven*. There are wolves, *lobos*, in the hills.'

'I love wolves,' I answered, more preoccupied with my sore feet and what I would eat that night.

Across the street was a café filled with youngsters, sipping beer and listening to music amid the noisy chatter of plans to come. Parents watched their infants in the playground, smiling encouragement at those young lives they had dedicated their own life to. I walked unnoticed past weary labourers, gathered at tables cluttered with ashtrays and phones and bottles. Wearing paint-spattered vests, they laughed and drank beer and slammed down playing cards. The hills beyond the village looked promising for that night's camp. As I walked towards them, I wished for a cold beer. I wished for friends.

Last Light

I WAS SCOUTING FOR a camping spot when I first heard it. Howling. Then guttural barking from the low, rocky ridge I had just crossed. Wolves! I thought of the old woman's warning, cocked my head to listen, and grinned.

It came again: the eerie howl of wild animals. The cries were closer this time. Fear overwhelmed my excitement.

Then I spotted them. They were not wolves but a pair of massive dogs. I was both disappointed and relieved. Pale and thickset, they trotted aggressively towards me through the long yellow grass, snarling with menace. This was the first time in my life I had been really frightened by dogs.

The dogs were huge – waist height – and heavier and stronger than I was. They could certainly outrun me and outfight me. They prowled closer. I backed away, flailing my flimsy hiking poles, shouting, trying to intimidate them. The dogs barely flinched. Drool sprayed from their jaws as they snarled. I kept retreating, resisting fleeing, taking care not to stumble, never breaking eye contact. This similarity with Laurie's journey I would rather have avoided. He described wild dogs that 'came slinking and snarling along the ridge' where he camped, 'hackles bristling against the moon'. He kept them at bay 'only by shouting, throwing stones, and flashing my torch in their eyes'.

'Please leave me alone. Please go away,' I pleaded in my mind, while screaming obscenities at the top of my voice. I did not know what to do.

I inched backwards, yelling, heart thumping. Eventually, I reached a small road. It offered an illusion of civilisation and safety, even though there was no traffic. To my relief, the dogs appeared to think the same. The road unsettled their confidence. They stopped barking and, after a minute of growling stand-off, they drifted away. Drained, I watched the dogs swagger back into the hills.

I withdrew my claim of loving wolves and hurried down the road to find somewhere to spend the night. Wolves, dogs, whatever: I was done with wilderness and wildlife for the day! I wanted tarmac and streetlights. It took a while for my legs to stop shaking as I strode through the dusk.

At last I reached the sanctuary of a pretty, one-street village whose locals were out for a stroll. In Spain, both bookends of the day are treasured. Dawn – birdsong and the world lemon-yellow – was cherished only by me, for I invariably had it to myself. It is the evening bookend – birds swirling home to roost in the last indigo light – that Spaniards enjoy. Couples, families, old folk: everyone was outside now, enjoying the company and the cooler air. I asked a man where the *fuente* was.

'First of all,' he replied, pointing at me with his stick, 'tell me who you are.'

'I come from England. I am walking through your country,

busking to pay my way. I like it here very much. Yesterday I earned enough to fill my pack with bread. I feel like the king of the world.'

'Would you like a cold beer?'

'*¡Señor, gracias! ¡AHORA soy el rey del mundo!* NOW I am the king of the world!'

I shrugged off my pack and sat beside the gentleman on the stone bench outside his home. He had lived here for 60 years. The air was rich with the fragrance of lavender. We sipped our beers in the dimming light, accompanied by a few old folk and two girls about 10 years old. The girls wanted to practise their English while they played with their Labrador puppy.

Whenever I met a child in those rural villages, I knew someone had sent them up from Madrid to spend the summer in the fresh air with their grandparents. It seemed a delightful tradition. The kids were let off the leash to entertain themselves with their friends, ride bikes, or curl up reading a book in an open doorway. A man with white hair, a red shirt and an awkward limp led a donkey past us. He returned shortly, donkeyless, and joined the conversation. I was urged to retell my 'wolf' story for him. My encounter with the *mastines* had already caused much amusement.

Later, I settled down to sleep on the soft grass beside the community-run bar, safe from snarling fangs. I looked at the waxing moon through half-closed eyes. The only sound was a lullaby of chirping insects. My day was finished.

But, alas, the locals' day was not. A bunch of elderly friends opened up the bar to drink and play cards. I stood up to explain myself.

'How lovely to have a community bar,' I said.

'It is, except we have no customers but us!' they laughed.

I wriggled back into my sleeping bag and listened, not to gentle crickets, but to raucous laughter, clinking glasses and the slamming of cards until well after midnight.

The next evening, after 25 miles of huff and puff, I made my home in a field of straw bales, far from the merest hint of wolf. Once night approaches, even in a country as safe as Spain, I always feel the primitive unease that Laurie described as 'that faint sour panic which seems to cling to a place until one has found oneself a bed'.

I tugged off my damp shirt and unpacked my bag. The sun was a crimson orb perched on the horizon. Lightning flashed to the south, and a storm wind blew, but fortunately it did not rain. I poured oats into my fire-blackened pan, added water and stirred in a mashed banana. I ate on a bale beneath the thunder and sunshine, then washed my pan, drank the dishwater and stuffed it back into my rucksack.

Sometime after dark, the bright lights of a combine harvester ripped me from sleep. I did not want the farmer to be alarmed at the sight of a body in his field, nor did I want him to harvest me. So I stood and approached the blazing lights and roaring rotors, squinting and waving and trying my best not to look like a scary weirdo. I greeted the surprised farmer and explained myself. He didn't mind me lying in his field, so I returned to my sleeping bag while the machine roared up and down through my dreams.

Treasure

BUSKING AT DUSK ALWAYS carried an optimistic vibe. The temperature was less vindictive, and there were more playing hours available before the streets emptied. In fact, the later I played, the better: this was Spain after all. The setting sun slanted shadows or blinding blasts of gold. The town filled with people in a strolling kind of mood. In street cafés and bars the last of the sunlight fell on golden beer, shining black hair and bowls of green olives.

The disadvantage of busking in the evening was that I was tired and needed to sleep. I wanted to flop onto a soft sofa in a dark room and eat pizza. Spending extra hours on my feet, even standing still, was wearing. And the impending darkness made me jittery. It played on my mind that I still needed to find somewhere safe to camp.

I walked along the main street searching for a place to busk. It was a town of stately old buildings and quiet alleys of bric-a-brac shops. My sore feet appreciated the smoothness of the paving stones. All around me were couples holding hands and toddlers chasing balloons. Families sipped wine

outside cafés fronted with stone columns, relaxing over beer
bottles cold with condensation, and picking at plates piled
with fried potatoes and slathered in ketchup. I felt irrelevant
and invisible. But everybody was about to know I was here.
I sighed and smiled. Here we go again. Then I raised the
violin to my shoulder and pulled the trigger.

> Tell me the tales that to me were so dear,
> Long, long ago, long, long ago . . .
> Let me forget that so long you have roved.

A musical parade interrupted me. I stepped back against
the wall to make way. I was as relieved as anyone to pause
from my eighth rendition of 'Long, Long Ago' and listen to
music played properly. I applauded the colourful performers
marching to a concert in the plaza. Now that I had dabbled
with music myself, I could better appreciate the skill necessary
to march in time, belting out a tune on the *gaita* – Spanish
bagpipes – while looking quite bored and angry.

After I resumed playing, a neatly dressed woman approached.
She was a piano teacher. She instructed me to keep practising
and pressed 60 cents into my hand. An old man, doddery on
his walking stick, fumbled in his purse and gave me 22 cents.
He had spotted my big rucksack and told me that he used to
hike a lot when he was young.

'*Caminar es atesorar,*' he said. 'Walking is like seeking
treasure. It's an old saying. You always find something out
there, don't you?'

I agreed with him. It was a nice proverb. We chatted about
my route through the hills.

'This walk of yours, you're really *viviendo su vida*, living your life!'

His reassurance boosted me more than his gift of money. But it was not true. Or, more accurately, it was no longer true. For 20 years, travelling had filled my life. But my wanderlust had become a hindrance since I became a father and my raging against confinement and loss of identity complicated life. Being pulled in two directions, wanting everything, enjoying nothing, going nowhere, I had gathered no treasure recently.

But now I was sorting myself out again, shrugging off the weight of dissatisfaction. I no longer regarded adventures as a panacea for my woes or the sum of who I was. This short walk would not resolve my dilemmas, *la noche oscura del alma*, but it was showing me the progress I had made in untangling the knots of my mind. This solid month of happiness gave me hope that, at last, I was perhaps beginning to *vivir mi vida* once again.

Coffee

SOMETIMES I APPROACHED VILLAGES down boulevards of rustling plane trees, stumbling in the afternoon heat, footsore, hungry, irritable. First impressions sway my judgement of a place. The unknown, with all its frustrations and delights, is alluring. Segovia, for example, which I discovered near the end of my walk, rose out of wheat fields, catching me unawares. There it is! Six hot air balloons, silhouetted and backlit, drifted right to left above the imposing cathedral, the mountains dark behind. Arrive in Zamora from the south, as Laurie did, and a graceful riverside town welcomes you, 'stacked on its rocky hill, a ripple of ochre roofs and walls, the river broad and dotted with islands and rapids'. Had I seen that, rather than the shopping centres, roundabouts and blocks of flats I spent hours trudging past from the north, I might have been more generous with my memory of the place.

Today, up on the red rocky ridge, perched on the blue skyline, stood Toro. I recognised it from the front cover of *As I Walked Out One Midsummer Morning*. Houses clutched the edge, 'like dried blood on a rusty sword'. Their windows and balconies looked far out over the sheer drop. I hoped for a profitable few hours with my violin but, like Laurie, 'clambering up to the town in the hard noon silence I was ready to find it deserted'. I paused halfway up the climb to catch my breath under the excuse of admiring the view. Then I turned and entered Toro, curious about what I would find. At the Church of San Lorenzo el Real, the repeating arches of its Mudéjar style nodded to centuries of Moorish influence. The plains of Castile rolled into the hazy distance, and the river I had followed curved away round wooded bends.

Arriving in a town where nobody knows my name might make it onto my list of favourite things to do. Whiling away an afternoon in a café certainly would. As my busking skills improved, I could occasionally invest in a short black coffee. I never dreamed my wealth might reach such extravagant heights. But that made it even more enjoyable to stagger through the fly screen, pushing the strings of beads aside and fleeing the sun, like Laurie. He, too, suffered from the heat 'in a state of developing madness, possessed by pounding deliriums of thirst'. He stumbled into a bar 'croaking, desperate with thirst. Somebody gave me some ice to suck. Then I was told to rest and cool off, while they asked me the usual questions: where I came from, where I was going.' Once I had answered those same questions, I ordered a small coffee and apologised that this was all I could afford. Then, flop. Head on table. Hot, damp, delirious.

One euro bought not only coffee but also permission to sit vacant and broken in the gloom, overstaying my welcome in an unobtrusive corner, hiding from the sun and charging my cameras. The usual customers in the usual church square café. Chattering old men, tumblers of beer, golden vermouth, *sol y sombra* – brandy and *anís*, cigarettes rasping voices and clouding the air. An old woman smoking and coughing, the trotter of a leg of *jamón* sticking out of her shopping trolley. Last year's calendar on the wall, last week's gossip in the air, yesterday's *tapas* on the counter. Dust dancing in the sunlight, settling in the shadows, *claroscuro*. A gold plastic clock above the bar ticking away the minutes of heat and my life. A gabbling TV game show ignored by everyone. Then the local news. Weather warnings issued in 28 of Spain's provinces: a dust cloud from the Sahara bringing 40-degree heat.

I slumped over a corner table, shoes and socks surreptitiously removed, feet throbbing. My pack and violin slumped on the floor beside me. I liked the pain as validation of a hard day. Some things seem destined never to change. I stirred my coffee treacle-thick with sugar. Bonus free calories. Sweet and sharp on my tongue, each sip tingling my nerves. Then I spread my diary and maps across the table, scheming and dreaming, calculating distances and routes, pottering through the afternoon's hottest hours.

Before leaving the café I pushed the acceptable limits of my one euro coffee investment. I slipped into the cramped toilet. Gambling on nobody coming in for a couple of minutes, I whipped off my shirt, squirted a handful of soap from the dispenser into my palms and sluiced my armpits in the tiny sink. Then I leaned forwards and washed my hair. I caught a glimpse of myself in the mirror, the first in a long time. I was russet, dripping, bristly. Ribs showing, torso milky-white. My face was weathered, and my eyes had sunk behind sunshine spokes. I noticed a brightening of the eyes and a sharpening of the cheek and jaw as my body and mind stiffened to the task, leaving behind the flabbiness of my ordinary life. I grinned at myself, a surprised flash of solidarity and companionship. I'm not alone. I've got me. Wherever I go, there I am.

Kindness

THE BARMAN MOVED SWIFTLY each time his wife carried a handful of dirty glasses into the kitchen. He sank a bottle of beer, furtive and fast, brushed the foam from his grey moustache and threw the bottle away before she returned. Whenever the barman went outside to clear tables, his young wife – her face smooth and not yet crumpled like her husband's – slipped money from the till, fed it into the fruit machine and returned to the bar in one continuous, bored movement. She had stopped expecting her luck to change, but she still hoped.

I sat observing, unobserved, the outsider peering into other lives while running from his own. The couple did not speak or look at each other. When they crossed paths, they recoiled to avoid touching. Each of them wishing for something different, keeping secrets, in a life they seemed unable to escape.

A steady turnover of paunchy, leathery men came to the café to drink a glass or two, eat *tapas* with a cocktail stick, bark out bursts of conversation, or sit in self-contained silence smoking cigars. They rubbed their fingers on a paper towel then dropped it on the floor before leaving. It was *la hora del vermut*, the traditional time for a quick drink before returning home to eat.

The barman gestured at empty seats as he moaned to me about the lack of money in the country. He blamed 'the Moors' – immigrants – who were flooding back into Spain to take over again, as they had done when they ruled here for 800 years. Outbreeding the native Spaniards, he said, taking all our jobs. He wiped the bar in disgust, but his cloth was dirty and the bar stayed grimy.

His wife, a Dominican immigrant, came out of the kitchen and surprised me with a plate of spicy potatoes, chicken wings and a large glass of iced water.

'*Toma este regalo para el viaje de mi parte.* A gift for your journey.'

She squeezed my shoulder and walked away. A wish, perhaps, that she could walk out of the door as easily as I could. A taste of vicarious freedom. Laurie, heat-exhausted, once slumped at a table with his head in his arms. A woman 'pushed some fried eggs before me, and poured me a glass of purple wine'. While the women murmured together, Laurie 'ate the honoured meal of the stranger'.

I pressed the chill of the glass to my heat-hammered head, aware she was watching me from behind the bar. When I turned my head she looked away and smoothed her skirt. The economics of a café giving away food made little sense. But giving more than is asked was perhaps an antidote to her frustrations, choosing to put kindness before resentment.

I remembered that I had not asked the man who gave me my very first coin for his name, just as I did not know this lady's. That was the way it was all summer. I was passed from town to town, coin to coin, by a chain of anonymous people, each offering a small gesture to a stranger that together contributed to something substantial. Yet how much easier it is to be kind to an interesting stranger than to our own family, or even to ourselves.

'What is your name?' I asked.

'Camila.' She folded her arms and glanced towards her husband.

'*Eso fue sabrosa.* That was delicious. *Gracias, Camila.*'

She smiled.

That evening I made sure to appreciate walking through the countryside, to look around and pay attention. Cows browsed idly, belly deep in soft grass. I swooshed through the long grass, thick with nettles and wild mint, then turned upwards through groves of sweet chestnut trees, their leaves glossy, their odour cloying. I passed small waterfalls and clear pools. A hare bolted across the meadow in front of me. The light was liquid, and the hills and woods dripped with colour.

Gambling

A DIFFERENT CAFÉ, DIFFERENT day, different Dominican. Paloma wore her unruly hair in a top knot, and everything made her smile. I sat at the bar and sipped my coffee, procrastinating while my batteries charged. Her son, Matías, told me he hadn't seen his father since moving to Spain eight years earlier. He was now 20. He rubbed his hands along the patterns shaved into the side of his head and looked rueful at the long separation.

When I tried to pay, Paloma waved my coin away and bombarded me with questions. I was her entertainment on a quiet afternoon. She gasped or laughed at every answer. It was a fun conversation. The customer sitting next to me, busy downing several glasses of wine, was interested in Laurie. I handed him my dog-eared book, apologising that I did not have a Spanish translation. I asked him how he rated my busking prospects.

'¿*Aqui?* Here?' he raised an eyebrow and sniffed. 'You won't make much in this town.'

Pessimists always bend me towards reckless optimism.

'It'll be easy!' I told him. 'I'm going to get rich tonight. I'll buy you a glass of wine later.'

'I bet you won't even earn five euros.' He emptied his glass.

'You're on! I'll bet you a euro.'

We shook hands on our bet, and I picked up my violin and headed out to play.

Some hours later, stubborn persistence carried me across the five euro threshold. I headed back to the café to collect my winnings. But my man had already left, much to Paloma's amusement. I splashed my hoard of coins down on the bar and recklessly ordered my second coffee of the day. Paloma applauded.

Though darkness was falling, I lingered with Paloma and Matías, cherishing their fleeting friendship. A contrast to the daily gloom I heard about the economy, it was refreshing to talk to these immigrants who looked at Spain through fresh eyes, grateful for the opportunities they saw and daring to be happy. It takes sacrifice and hard work and courage to start a new life in a foreign country.

I confided that I was missing my family and found the busking nerve-wracking.

'You can't be crying,' they insisted. '*Tú has elegido este viaje.* You chose this journey.'

By the time I had walked out of town, I couldn't be fussy about my camping spot. In the last glimmer of light, I crawled under an abandoned shipping container behind a warehouse. My new home offered expansive views of the river valley beyond a silhouetted digger. I paused from writing my diary to improve the shelter, blocking a draft that seeped beneath the metal walls. Then, house-proud, I settled down to sleep.

The Art of Busking

AS THE WEEKS PASSED, I grew fond of the Spanish. They were chatty but not nosey, polite but not reserved, and the old folk were much cheerier than pensioners back home. They were amicable and supportive, if only through smiles and murmured imprecations. I was touched by how encouraging everyone was of my bad violin playing.

I learned that there was more to the art of beguiling my Spanish audiences than just playing tunes. I discovered the importance of positioning: where to bottleneck and funnel pedestrians, avoiding spots where people were too preoccupied to give of their time or money, or sites so crowded that everyone thought someone else would be the one to donate. I paid close attention to every person who walked past. I focused on their attitude and clothes, their expressions and body language. I began to develop a sense for who was likely to give a coin or two.

Young people were hopeless. Glued to their phones or chatting with friends, they didn't even notice me. Those under 40 were too busy to be distracted. Parents with infants looked too frazzled to stop, unless a toddler showed an interest in me, in which case I provided a brief respite. Grandparents with youngsters were often good for a coin; strolling old couples, too. It surprised me how frequently somebody gave money when I was not playing, whether I was setting up or chatting.

Anyone whistling. Anyone smiling.

Nobody looking at their phone.

People who held eye contact or returned a smile.

I rated my chances highly whenever an attractive woman walked by. They tended to disagree.

In my experience, men over 50 gave the most frequently, though younger donors gave more. My most regular supporters were male pensioners. They listened only for the seconds they were passing, dropped a coin without breaking stride and continued on their way.

Most people donated between 50 cents and a euro. A few sprinkled a consoling confetti of tiny denomination coins. They sounded fabulous as they landed and I gushed my thanks, but it took a lot of copper to buy a loaf.

Tiredness eventually beat me, and I called it quits for the night in a children's playground, lured by the triple wonders of soft grass to sleep on, a table to sit at and even a tap offering running water. It was the perfect campsite, even without the swings and slides.

To crown it all, I discovered a discarded tub of pork scratch-ings in the rubbish bin. Whether the thought of eating pork scratchings from a bin repulses you or you share my jubilation probably depends on whether or not you have ever been hungry and broke. This trumped a day of magnificent eating, for earlier I had found half a baguette on a roadside verge, sun-baked, hard as a rusk and with a hint of diesel.

How my wealth compares to the local population's affects my behaviour on journeys. I hide my riches – cameras, a second pair of socks – in poor countries to minimise alienation, temptation of theft, or crowds of astonished onlookers. I feel uneasy and set apart. When people appear to be richer than I am – something I experienced cycling through Europe and North America – I feel like a misfit, half envious, half resentful. In Spain, however, I felt at ease. I didn't have much cash. I was scavenging in bins. But it was by choice. By and large, I was on the same financial and educational level as everyone here. I could chat in their language. I was confident that I could belong here, that holy grail for the lonely nomad.

I chewed my pork scratchings and rubbery carrots as I waited for the last of the children to leave the playground so that I could lie down to sleep by the swings without appearing too weird.

Alone

THE MAP SHOWED THAT the coming days would be
isolated. But my pack was heavy with cold water, and a floury
loaf stuck out of the top. I would be fine: the last town had
treated me well. I walked away from all the people I had
connected with, all those who had donated or smiled. I would
never meet them again. They would soon forget me. Leaving
and wiping the slate clean. Nothing left behind, everything
ahead of me.

I left the shaded streets and returned to the dusty tracks,
the sky big, the buildings receding until only the church tower
lingered in view over my shoulder. I walked towards the next
small town waiting under the hot sun for me. Although, of
course, it was not waiting for me. Nothing is. It is another
conceit of solo travel that the world revolves around you and
should give a damn. As Laurie wrote when he left Slad back
in 1935, 'I was excited, vain-glorious, knowing I had far to
go; but not, as yet, how far. As I left home that morning and
walked away from the sleeping village, it never occurred to
me that others had done this before me.'

I was out of the hills now and onto the Castilian plain, surrounded by sunflowers. Some fields stood heads up in joyful reverence, like a festival crowd. In other acres the flowers slumped like the weary armies who marched this parched land before me. For the first time on the trip I shuffled along, kicking up dust and dreaming of the end – of Madrid, money, fresh clothes. I was tired of being a stranger. I craved music and a good book. I was underfed and overwalked.

To pass the time, I daydreamed about all the happy times I had shared with Sarah, times of laughter and peace, not wordless tension. I remembered us dancing together at a wedding in India and swimming in misty Lake Geneva. I pictured her tanned and laughing in a short white dress at a birthday party. I held my mind for a while to a hope that my kids may now be old enough and bold enough to enjoy jumping into a river with me. And still the sunflowers whispered as I walked, my only companion for those shimmering miles. 'I felt I was treading the rim of a burning wheel, kicking it behind me step-by-step, feet scorched and blistered yet not advancing an inch and pinned forever at this sweltering spot.'

I detoured into a village to fill my bottles. An old man in a beret with a single fang tooth gave me directions. I sat under the *fuente* and let the water douse my head and shirt.

'Where there is water, there is action,' said a disgruntled, hot workman tasked to hose down the empty concrete plaza. It seemed wasteful on these arid plains. He hailed from Galicia, the land of a thousand rivers, and hated living far from the ocean.

'There's no fishing here, no sea, nothing. Just shooting with guns for fun. Bleurgh!'

*   *   *

Across the plain, a train grew larger. I urged the driver to hoot me as it passed, my arm hauling down the imaginary lever for a giant horn. This is a childish pleasure I indulge on every foreign trip. At home, I am expected to be too grown up to implore train drivers to sound their horns. But I am a cheerier fellow in the rest of the world. The train did hoot, though meekly. I prefer the exuberant blasts you get in India.

Mild amusements are brief distractions from the enormity of being alone on the road. No other human for miles. Nobody asking or answering questions, diverting me from myself. No roof over my head. No separation between me and the sun, the wind and the stars. One of the lasting problems with walking a solitary path is that few people can empathise. When you cannot hear the music someone is dancing to, you're inclined to consider them insane. And going away puts you at a distance even when you return. Even those you love will always stand apart. Many think you're mad or ask 'what's the use?'

Aloneness is a rare commodity these days. Even the small act of turning off your phone is inconceivable for most working people. We are never disconnected. Most of humanity lives squashed together in cities. You can be lonely in a city, but you cannot be alone. You can be lonely in a family, too, though with children you are rarely by yourself.

The fine line between loneliness and solitude depends upon your state of mind. Some days it seems glorious to follow my own path. Other days it is overwhelmingly sad to walk among streets filled with strangers. But being alone in a landscape rarely feels like emptiness or loss for me. Rather, the solitude is a physical presence that restores me like a long sleep. I can then go back to the family fray better equipped to give of myself. Going away purely in order to return reminds me of Tolstoy's tale of the poor beggar. The man spent his days pleading for help, longing for his life to change. He was so mired in his gloom that he never noticed that the box he sat on every day was stuffed with gold.

Fiesta

'THERE WILL BE *CHURROS!* And *patatas fritas!*' a boy in a Real Madrid shirt assured me with a smile.

Cheered by this tip-off about a nearby fiesta and an opportunity to busk, I changed route, veering southwest towards a church tower shimmering across the fields.

I arrived in the small town by early evening, ready to work. I was hungry. The plaza, however, was peculiarly empty. I groaned once again at the different concepts of time in Spain and Britain. An hour later there was still no sign of a party, except that the *churros* van had arrived. Its bright lights and aroma carried the promise that maybe something might happen if only I could stay awake long enough. My stomach rumbled at the smell of food, even if the woman was smoking while she fried the *churros*. A Romanian approached me and begged for money to buy *churros* for her daughter. The little girl was dressed as a Disney princess. Lucy had the same turquoise dress at home.

'Sorry, I have nothing,' I said, truthful for once in brushing off such a request.

Even at this late hour the day's heat radiated from the pavement I was sitting on, making me sweat. I was irked at waiting for nothing to happen. I wanted to be sleeping, not violining. After another hour I decided to give up, go to sleep in a field, then return at lunchtime to busk and buy food.

I walked past the town hall, painted red and yellow and adorned with the national and regional flags. Turning down a street towards open countryside I met a straggle of dusty drunks dressed in white, with red sashes tied around their waists. Round another corner, and suddenly the place was packed with the bubbling, chattering aftermath of a party.

I was so accustomed to everything happening late in Spain that it had not occurred to me the fiesta might already be bouncing in a different part of town. I had missed dozens of mad men and bulls racing through the streets as the climax to the fiesta. Driven by confusion and fear, the bulls run hard and fast. Driven by booze and testosterone, crowds of men run among the bulls, trying to get close enough to gloat, but without getting gored. I was disappointed to miss this most Spanish of spectacles and furious at myself. Then someone offered me a *bocadillo de chorizo* from the communal barbecue. I declined.

'*Es gratis,*' he said.

The smoky grill smelled delicious and reminded me how hungry I was. I accepted the free sandwich with a weary smile.

'*¿Quieres vino?* Would you like some wine as well? Wow, you drank that fast. Another sandwich, more wine?'

I stood eating absentmindedly while the crowd waded homewards around me through a mess of discarded plastic beer glasses. Then a young woman dashed over to me, wide-eyed.

'Is you Aleestar?' she asked, in English.

Surprised, I confirmed that I was.

'My friend want to speak with you!'

I was confused. Nobody knew that I had diverted to this town.

'*¿Quién me esta buscando?* Who is looking for me?'

'My friend Marcos. He is a traveller, like you,' she explained, returning to Spanish. 'It is incredible that you are here. He is going to be so happy.'

The mystery woman had clearly been drinking. She began texting on her phone, muttering to herself as she typed.

I established that Marcos had been following my adventure on Facebook. He had briefed his friends to keep an eye out for me as my walk moved in his direction. I should be easy to spot – or hear – if I busked in any of their towns. Marcos was hurrying to meet me now.

But it was late. I was exhausted. I was sulking about missing the fiesta and not in the mood to chat. And I resented this intrusion into my peaceful anonymity. I had uploaded a short video from my phone most days, but I never looked at any of the comments which followed. I wanted to share my story, but without being connected or beholden to the internet. It was a compromise I had thought hard about. Transmitting snippets of film but not receiving any messages from the outside world felt acceptable to me. I knew that people along my route would probably be offering beds and assistance. On other trips this has been a welcome part of the experience. But this time I did not want help. If nothing else, it was an unfair advantage over Laurie. A month without email or social media was one of my favourite parts of the whole experience. I had become tired of the blurring between my real and online worlds.

The crowd had thinned and I had almost finished my sandwich. I began making excuses.

'I'm sorry. I don't have time to stay. I have a long way to walk.'

But she clutched my arm and begged me to wait just a little longer, hanging on for her friend. We did a little back and forth tugging. But then Marcos arrived, out of breath. He had been running. He was about my age, with cropped, dark hair.

Having followed my walk online since the beginning, Marcos was astonished that I had happened to come directly to his small town. Some of his friends gathered now from the fiesta, a little drunk and very friendly. Marcos told them about me and how he had tracked me down. He appeared to be a decent guy, not some weird 'fan'. Plus the chorizo was magnificent, and the wine was hitting me hard. So I soon softened. And, actually, the thought of a day off was tempting . . .

So I asked myself, 'What would Laurie do?'

'Marcos, you are very kind. I'd love to come and stay at your house. *Gracias.*'

To my amusement, Marcos jumped and punched the air. He clapped me on the shoulder and insisted on carrying my rucksack for me.

'Fantastic. You will be my guest.'

Respite

ONE EVENING LAURIE PASSED his hat round a café after playing to the sunset crowds. The poet Roy Campbell and his wife, Mary, happened to be there. Mary asked Laurie, '"D'you like risotto?" And said she was sure there was more than enough if I cared to go home with them for supper.'

Laurie was delighted to accept. 'Supper was served in the patio under the open sky, with several bottles of local wine, and I found myself sitting down to a well-laid table for the first time in almost two months.'

Marcos lived with his mum, and she was mortified at an unannounced visitor arriving in her kitchen.

'The spare room is not prepared!'

Helena hid a dirty coffee cup in the sink.

'Oh, Marcos! Why didn't you warn me? Just turning up like this? Honestly!'

She flicked a tea towel at her son.

'The house is such a mess!'

Marcos and I grinned at each other. My mum would have reacted the same way. The house was spotless. On the short walk to his home, Marcos had already told me about his own travels by bicycle and his reluctance to settle for work that bored him. Enough for me to know that we would get on well.

I tried to reassure Helena, as she clucked and fussed, that everything was perfect.

'I have not slept in a bed for weeks, so I'm just delighted to be here. Please don't worry.'

At this Helena threw Marcos a look of disbelief. Who was this tramp her son had dragged home? Marcos chuckled and wisely steered me away from his mother, showing me upstairs for my first shower in Spain.

Fragrant and fresh once again, I headed out for the evening with Marcos, dressed in borrowed clothes and relaxing into my unexpected holiday. Because I had no money I had pretended that I wanted to rest rather than go out. But Marcos had insisted.

'I want you to meet my friends. Don't worry: I am buying the beer. I know how bad your violin playing is! Please leave it in the house.'

The warm night air was full of jasmine and cicadas. I felt excited to be going out, for conversations and music. Cold beers, fireworks flashing and high spirits as the summer fiesta drew to a close. We joined Marcos' friends at an outdoor bar. They were laughing, shouting and teasing each other. Everyone knew everyone, and people kept joining and leaving the conversation. I grew shy among them all, with their clean, stylish clothes and gabbling Spanish. But then someone handed me a beer and I squeezed onto the table and relaxed.

Marcos introduced his friend Elizabeth. She wanted to cycle

to Santiago but her boyfriend was reluctant for her to go. They turned to me for my opinion. I tried not only to remain diplomatically neutral but also to keep my eyelids open. I was not accustomed to either beer or midnight.

When I am a passing stranger, close communities like this feel idyllic. If I lived there, I suspect I would grow restless, but that night it felt perfect. With a cold beer on a warm evening, the sense of 'sonder' was almost overwhelming – that occasional realisation that every single person is living a life as rich and tangled as your own. We were all experiencing this exact moment, but in unique ways. So many fears and hopes and stories. Sonder comes on strong when I travel, drifting into lives I could not have imagined, shaking hands with people I never knew existed. And now here we were all together, our lives all containing this hour.

There are so many villages waiting in the world that I will never explore, lively with street music, lit by bright bulbs as moths flit among the ideas and arguments and music. All these places are mere words on a map until you bump into them (if they are on maps at all, and many of the best places are not). And then it all springs to life: the beer bottles perched on pool tables, balls clicking and jukebox playing, or bubbling conversations round fragrant sheesha pipes, sundowner drinks in noisy shebeens and under the slow fans of outback pubs, masala chai and Bollywood tunes at grimy roadside tea stands.

When you travel, the world becomes real and three-dimensional, impossibly vivid. All those evenings under the stars, the groups of friends, old women or young bucks, the married couples and blind dates, fluttering nerves and new perfume, sharing lives and dreams, companionable silence, belonging, imagining, clinking glasses amid the swirls of blue cigarette smoke and raising of toasts. Realising that I cannot be part of it all is one of my biggest sadnesses as my travels draw to a close. It haunts me that I will only ever scratch the surface.

I leaned back and gazed at the stars, letting the conversation drift away. My head swirled. I travel precisely for times like these, yet being on the move meant I lacked these precious gifts in my own life: the strength of community and friendship. To be everywhere is to be nowhere. To try to have everything is a certain way to end up with nothing. I envied this crowd of mates, gathered together where they had all lived their lives. I was grateful to have been welcomed by them, a well-loved stranger offered an unexpected respite from the road. Roy and Mary Campbell had done the same for Laurie. He wrote, '[I] was treated with a matter-of-fact kindness which surprised and charmed me. I'd arrived from nowhere, but nobody bothered me with questions; I was simply accepted and given the run of the house.'

I slept terribly that night – the bed too soft, the room too warm. But it was delicious to wake at dawn, as usual, and then roll over and fall back to sleep. Instead of walking, as I had done every day, I passed the day drinking coffee and lazing about. I felt listless and hungry, a lassitude that always dumps down on me on a rest day. Marcos and I spent hours chatting at the kitchen table while Helena plied me with sliced cucumbers, *lomo* and *pan con tomate*.

Helena had warmed to me once I got cleaned up and wanted to make a fuss. She showed me the many horsemanship trophies her late husband had won, lifting one down to polish it with her sleeve. She talked me through the family photos framed on the bookshelves, much to her son's embarrassment. Her favourite was a family gathering at her golden wedding anniversary. I marvelled at what an extraordinary amount of time together that represented. Since her husband's death, Helena had taken up painting. Her improvement was astonishing. I dream of being able to draw, so I asked Helena what the secret was.

'*La práctica.*'

At some point Marcos and I cycled to the local *bodega* to fill a couple of empty lemonade bottles with white wine. Then, in the evening, we pedalled down to the river for a picnic with his girlfriend Victoria, and Elizabeth. What luxury to glide at the speed of a bicycle, rather than the plodding of a pedestrian!

Marcos laid a cloth beneath the trees and spread it with his mum's *tortilla de patatas*, crunchy peppers, chorizo, wedges of watermelon and wine. Other local families were also picnicking by the river, and Marcos knew them all. It was an evening of hugs, kisses, backslaps and laughter. Village life at its best provides an extended family.

Marcos and Victoria told me about their adventures, cycling trips together through Britain and Denmark. They were animated about their future plans, and I enjoyed not needing to talk about my trip. We all tried to encourage Elizabeth to ride to Santiago. She was suffering the familiar tug between the wild heart wanting to be free and the tame heart that feels safer at home. Elizabeth wanted to do the ride solo but was worried by how little she knew, and doubted whether she could cope. Those concerns were also precisely why she wanted to try.

I have had this conversation so many times, with so many people, going all the way back to the very first time, when it was with myself. Back then, I did not dare to stay, so I went. I am certain I made the right decision by going, though it didn't turn out to be the easy decision. I have listened to the confessions and excuses of so many people afraid of taking the first step towards where they want to be. It comes down, in the end, to little more than summoning the guts to begin. Concentrate on getting started, then afterwards you can think about everything else. It is a simple solution. Simple but not easy. The best, most straightforward, scariest advice that I share comes from adventurer Audrey Sutherland: 'go simple, go solo, go now'.

We cycled back along the bumpy track, wine-wobbly and laughing. With no lights on our bikes, the Milky Way arched serenely above us. A shooting star streaked improbably through the story, plummeting to earth in front of us. We whooped and made wishes. I wished simply to remember this moment.

Chorizo

AS I PACKED TO leave the next morning, Helena fingered the sewing repairs I had made on my shirt. I could see she was unimpressed. She was not at all confident that I could take care of myself. And she hadn't even heard me play the violin! Helena's final offering, after so much kindness, was a large chorizo. She handed it to me in the hallway as I buckled up my rucksack.

'Here, put this in your bag. *Aquí tienes, toma esto.* You will need it later.'

My appetite, not to mention my manners, suggested I should have accepted the gift with thanks. Instead, I declined Helena's chorizo and then spent most of the day's hot miles dreaming of it. I am sure the self-imposed pressures I lay upon myself are not good for my sanity! Helena was bewildered. Why would a hungry, hard-up violinist turn down food, particularly when I had already eaten half the contents of her fridge?

I know that I can walk a long way, carry a heavy pack and sleep on the ground (though a donkey can do all those things better than I can). What I did not yet know was whether I could make it to Madrid by busking alone. The hospitality of a rest day was one matter, but on the road everything had to depend on the violin. If I didn't busk successfully, I would fail. This gave the journey its purpose and piquancy.

I politely refused the chorizo and hugged Helena and Marcos goodbye.

It was a small and pedantic statement of intent, but I was pleased with my decision. Later, I played my violin in a tatty village with a grassy plaza shaded by half a dozen saplings. I earned a few euros. And as I ate my evening meal in a pine forest – a tin of lentils with thin slices of my own chorizo – I hoped that Helena and Marcos were sitting in their garden, enjoying a glass of *Verdejo* and the chorizo, the sunshine scented with ripening tomatoes.

This walk was not about walking. It was about earning the chorizo.

Cassiopeia

MARCOS HAD TOLD ME that open fires were banned during Spain's tinder-dry summer months. My evenings would be lonelier without one. As I had not brought a stove, I could no longer cook. This forced me to become more imaginative with my meals, rather than eating stodgy rice every day. I passed a pleasant couple of hours musing how to eat a tomato.

Perhaps I should eat it like an apple, I thought. I was thirsty and craved the juiciness. Then I considered slicing the tomato for a sandwich, tangy juices complementing crusty bread. But when tea time finally arrived, high in wooded hills, I had settled on a new plan. By now I was starving, and quantity was my priority.

I diced the tomato with my penknife, then mixed it with half an onion saved from the previous day. I ripped bread into small chunks, stirred everything together and topped the pan right up to the brim with water. Instant gazpacho!

The sun set through a fronded window of branches and long grass while I ate. Birds descended to roost in the trees, and the temperature fell. The hills turned purple as the night settled in with cicadas and silhouettes. The ground was soft with a thick layer of pine needles. Darkness, out here, felt not like a time to scurry for home, but rather a slow, steady signal that I *was* home for the night. I stretched my tarp over my sleeping bag and secured it to trees. One tent peg pinged away from its corner into the wood, leaving me with only three, plus a twig, for the rest of the trip.

I awoke chilled. The cicadas were silent, the evening fragrance had gone. I felt small in the darkness and seeping cold. Cassiopeia had rotated round the North Star, and a carpet of mist lay across the wood. I burrowed deeper into the sleeping bag, pulling it right up over my head.

My rule of thumb for packing for a trip is that, on the coldest nights, sleeping in all my clothes, I should wake shivering a couple of times, then roll over and fall back to sleep. That means I am carrying the right amount of gear. If I am never cold, I have too many clothes or my sleeping bag is too thick. But if I lie freezing – teeth chattering, toes numb, doing press-ups in my sleeping bag, waiting miserably for sunrise – then I have taken minimalism a step too far.

At the first smear of dawn, bone-cold and dew-wet, I gave up on sleep. Shivering, I started to do some exercises to get the blood flowing: star jumps and running on the spot. I hoiked my pack onto my back with a groan and hurried through the wet grass. My hands were numb, and my breath ballooned.

It was a real relief when I welcomed the first strike of sunlight on my face after a long hour of shiver walking. I closed my eyes, enjoyed the warm glow and sang aloud 'Here Comes the Sun'. I have greeted the sunrise with this song every morning on my adventures since one freezing dawn, long ago, high in the Andes. It runs like a seam through the best days of my life.

> Here comes the sun, little darling.
> Here comes the sun.
> It's all right, It's all right.

Party

TWO BROTHERS SPOTTED MY hiking poles and the violin on my pack as I searched for midday shade. They beckoned me over to their café table and asked where I was going. They were in their early twenties and killing time on a family holiday while their parents went for a hike. They invited me to join them at their table. I was happy to rest my legs for a while. My stool wobbled on the cobbles, and I shuffled round to get out of the sun.

The younger brother, Leo, cradled a guitar in his lap. He had raven feathers tattooed on his forearms and a mop of curly, dark hair. Leo was eager to get out and travel the world with his guitar. He scribbled thoughts in his diary, practised his chords and grilled me for travel book recommendations.

'Oh God, I just want to go everywhere!' Leo answered in anguish, when I asked him his plans.

The elder brother, Rafa, was calmer. He sipped his wine, rolled cigarettes and smiled at his chattering brother. Their parents returned about an hour later. They were hot from their walk, and urgently ordered Cokes ('*con hielo*') and lit cigarettes. After introductions and explanations María began peppering me with questions about my life. She was a friendly lady, nervous about Leo's wanderlust, but wanting to be supportive of her boy as he flew the nest. María ordered me a beer as if to urge me to talk, to stay a while and enlighten her. The waiter served a platter of ribs and chicken wings and María insisted I share them with the family. I tried to reassure her about her restless son.

I reasoned that wanting to explore when you were young was a robust impulse. María shouldn't worry about that. The lessons from those travels would serve Leo well in the decades of work that lay ahead of him. I did not regret a single journey I had taken, but there were one or two it pained me to have missed. There was time for adventure, time for work, time for family. It was possible to do it all, though hard to achieve at the same time. Life has its many parts and all play their role in a fulfilling life. It was healthy to move through them without regret for missed opportunities, or with a yearning for chapters past. By now, I was not sure whether I was talking to María or myself! But I did promise her that I still phoned my mum. María called for a fresh bottle of beer.

The bar owner came outside to say hello to the family. He was one of those pushy, loud men with moustaches who talk a lot, slap people on the back and don't listen to anyone's answers. He commandeered Leo's guitar and began to play. He was annoying, but he was good, and he knew how to raise a crowd.

Soon all of our table, and those nearby, were singing along. I did not know the songs, but I was filled with such delight. Three girls and a guy staggered from the bar, drawn by the music, and started dancing on the cobbles. The drunkest girl, Concha, collared me and hauled me, laughing, to my feet. She slurred the lyrics loudly in my ear as we danced. Other people joined us. A group of strangers, linked in a circle as friends, dancing together in the sunny street. Late one night Laurie was slumped in a dance hall when a girl summoned him to dance. 'What with my blistered feet, and the beer in my head, it was as much as I could do to stand up. But the girl took charge – she just wrapped her damp arms round me, propped me snugly erect with her bosom, and away we went.'

Then somebody suggested I should play a song. They had spotted the violin on top of my rucksack. I resisted, much as I loved the idea, for I knew I was not good enough to hold a tune for a crowd. The more I protested, however, the louder the clamour grew. I continued to try to wriggle out of the inevitable, even as I picked up my violin and tightened the bow. I laughed nervously. When musicians protest about 'not being very good', you don't believe them. You assume they are being modest. People quickly believed me.

The guitarist did his best to steer us all through 'Guantanamera' at my ponderous speed, with Leo providing backing on his mouth organ. But the harsh reality was that I was nowhere near good enough. Leo's mum looked taken aback at how bad I was. I had told her that I was paying my way through Spain by busking. The rhythm and pace imposed by a guitar and singers was entirely beyond me. I simply could not keep up. My incompetence amused me, but I was disappointed. Playing at a street party would have been my musical pinnacle, the perfect opportunity to live the Laurie Lee dream. But I failed, except in raising some laughs. I did not want to kill the atmosphere, so after a few frustrating minutes I conceded defeat, packed away my violin and returned to waltzing with woozy girls.

The afternoon slipped by, the sun's heat softened and it came time to leave. The group chose a song for me, 'Adiós Corazón,' to see me on my way. Everyone sang, our arms around each other's shoulders in a tight circle. After a round of hugs and a declaration of love from Concha – who by now could barely stand – I was off, walking down the hill and leaving the music behind. I stole one more glance over my shoulder, one final wave. And then I marched out of town down the middle of the road, singing and stamping my hiking poles. It was a good job I'd only had two beers.

The sunlit road called me on. I had nowhere to be but here. The miles melted before me. Laurie would have approved of the day. Having squandered and spoiled almost a decade, the joy of these days ran deep. It was a balm to be in love with the world and my life once again.

Forest

THE LANDSCAPE CHANGED STEADILY as I walked
south through Castile. Behind me lay swathes of wheat fields,
plunging valleys of eucalyptus and crowds of sunflowers. It
is astonishing that, even on foot, a tiny human being can make
his way across sizeable spans of the planet – fuelled only by
banana sandwiches – yet with such slowness that you watch
a butterfly flexing its wings, catch a falling leaf, mind not to
step on that flower.

I walked now on sandy tracks through pine forests. The
forest was airy and peaceful with the tang of resin, 'a fresh
green smell as sweet as menthol'. Many trees had been 'slashed
with a pattern of fishbone cuts . . . bleeding gum into little
cups', just as they had when Laurie was here. They stood tall
and slender, with broad, flat crowns. The ground was strewn
with heavy cones, bigger than my fist. Cicadas whirred in the
branches. Each fell silent as I approached, like a workman
pausing his drill, looking up, mopping his brow and watching
me pass. His curiosity satisfied, he lowers his head and resumes
work.

I passed grazing deer, basking snakes and perched eagles. Little birds flitted among the trees and lizards scuttled across the fine sand, leaving tiny footprints and a trailing tail line. Barbed seeds stuck in my socks. I stopped to pluck them out. Minutes later they were full again. I concentrated instead on not concentrating on them. Stumbling upon an isolated home in a clearing, I knocked on the door to ask for water. Nobody was home so I helped myself from the outside tap. Emboldened, I then sat on their patio chair and made a banana sandwich, feeling like Goldilocks.

Then, one morning when the light was clean, a silhouetted outline of mountains soared above the horizon for the first time, 'a purple haze above the quivering plain – the first sign of the approaching Sierras. After the monotonous wheat fields, it was like a landfall, the distant coastline of another country, and, as I walked, it climbed steadily till it filled half the sky – the immense east–west barrier of the Guadarramas.'

Beyond those last blue mountains lay Madrid. Both the mountains and the end of my journey stood ready and waiting.

Permission

TWO RIVERS, THE ERESMA and the Clamores, hugged the town close and cinched it into position. The streams had bustled down from the mountains I was heading towards. Trees gleamed like sea glass above the crook of silver water. Segovia's Gothic cathedral and *alcázar*, the fortress, dominated the skyline with 'mediaeval walls standing sharp in the light' like the bow of a ship. One side was in shadow and the other honey-lit by low sunshine. The cathedral's domes and spires cascaded upwards to an imposing bell tower almost a hundred metres high. For five centuries its pealing bells had exalted the Virgin Mary down to the people.

Such riches ought to be enough for any town, yet I barely gave them a second look. For I was eager only to see Segovia's famous Roman aqueduct. I hurried through the old streets towards it, filled with anticipation. The aqueduct marched from the distant hills into the heart of the town. I dropped my rucksack at the base of its arches and stared. The massive granite masonry dwarfed me.

The aqueduct towered overhead, casting long shadows,

though no longer on the 'small black pigs running in and out
of shop doorways' that Laurie remembered. The only piglets
I saw were on photographs outside tourist restaurants adver-
tising *Cochinillo de Segovia*, the city's iconic dish of roast
suckling piglet, served whole and so tender that the meat is
carved with a plate not a knife.

Segovia's aqueduct has carried water from the hills into the
city for 2,000 years, an impressive return for a structure built
without mortar. I admired the boldness of those who began
the project, knowing what expense and difficulty lay ahead.
Unless, that is, the legend is true. The legend that Lucifer
himself built 'the devil's bridge' in just one dark night to win
a girl's soul. But *el puente del diablo* proved too great a feat,
even for the devil. Satan failed to fix the final stone before the
first rays of the morning sun struck, and so the girl's soul was
saved.

Swifts fizzed through the aqueduct's arches as I tuned my
violin. Tourists, less graceful, milled around on the ground
where Laurie once spent the night. These were the first foreign
tourists I had encountered in Spain. I hurried to get among
them, like a fisherman coming upon a rich shoal. Asian tour
groups paraded with selfie sticks. I heard Americans. They
wore college t-shirts and trainers, and clutched iPhones and
bottles of drinking water. There were wealthy Indian families
sipping from huge McDonald's cups, Spanish retirees and
eastern European hawkers. I was going to earn so much! I
was definitely going to eat chorizo tonight – maybe even ice
cream! I was greedy to play to these crowds with time on
their hands and cash to burn.

It was a disastrous session. I played for hours without
earning a penny. For all eyes were on the aqueduct, all thoughts

on group photos and selfies. Hundreds of people ignored me all morning, licking ice creams, fixated on sightseeing and oblivious to everything else. A tour group poured from a coach behind their leader and her little flag. They surrounded me, jabbering loudly, talking right across my face as though I was not even there. So I unleashed a torrent of discordant noise with my violin. Even then not one of the herd noticed. Their thoughts were only on their guide and where they would be fed. It was unsettling to become invisible.

But one person did see me that morning: a young Romanian distributing flyers. He urged me to play louder and tried to tempt me with a flyer.

'Special offer! Today only!'

I sighed. Even my chorizo dreams were fading, let alone having a meal in his restaurant. He wished me luck and went back to work. Later, he circled behind me, dropped a euro in my case and scurried away. I hastened after him to return the coin, for he was working hard and earning little. But he insisted I keep it.

I had a long conversation with a wealthy couple in their fifties, well-groomed and handsome. They lapped up the story of Laurie. My hike astounded them, they were impressed by my wild camping and they praised my entrepreneurial busking bravery. The woman asked me to play them a song before they went for lunch. This was the lucky break my day needed.

I played *The Muppet Show* theme tune as well as I could for them. They laughed, clapped and dug into their pockets. Success at last! I hummed as they took out their wallets, the day's hunger solved. I would buy the Romanian an ice cream, too, I decided. But between them, the couple gave me just 25 cents. My proud side wanted to return the money. Four measly coins after all the time we had talked. But my hungry side urged me to shut up and be grateful. I wished the couple '*buen provecho*', handed them the 'Special Offer!' flyer and concluded that it was not my lucky day.

Then: flashing blue lights! My neck prickled a warning instinct. The police. A squeeze of adrenalin. I quickly lowered my violin. A pair of policewomen on mopeds summoned me. Mirror shades, leather gloves, ponytails beneath the helmets. There must have been a tip-off, for they had come here specifically to deal with me. I walked over to them holding my violin, trying to decide whether it would help my cause to be able to understand Spanish or not.

'No permit, no play,' they began, sternly. 'You are not allowed to be here.'

I feigned innocence and apologised.

'Too many buskers . . . You are very poor quality . . .'

I dreaded that I was about to be fined.

'This is a big problem in our town. You must have permission.'

I lowered my eyes, contrite and worried. The police would not accept that I had no money except for the coins in my violin case.

'If you leave now, there will be no further action. You must come back tomorrow to apply for a permit at the *ayuntamiento*.'

As I exhaled with relief, I noticed my reflection in their sunglasses. I looked like a hobo. I grinned.

I laughed as I walked out of Segovia, heading for the mountains. I wasn't going to hang around for a permit I couldn't afford. There was always another village to play in, a new horizon to look towards. Nothing about this walk could keep me down for long. The pack on my back, food for the coming days and a few litres of water were the only weights I had to bear. I had always wanted to be a hobo. I mythologised the lifestyle and the spirit. Only recently did I learn that 'hobo' is short for 'homeward bound'.

Last Days

AND SO THE DAYS passed, and together they built the journey. Miles became memories. Days become a life. I could not remember when I had last felt this consistently happy. 'I'd been almost a month on the road; a month of vintage weather . . . I'd been glad to be back on my solitary marches, edging mindlessly from village to town, sleeping in thickets, in oases of rushes, under tall reeds, to the smell of water.'

Soothing hot feet in cold streams, dozing beneath gnarled cork trees, swatting flies, grumbling at the slowness of pedestrian miles, rolling out my sleeping bag somewhere new. 'The extravagant quality of being free on a weekday', and the additional enjoyment of jumping naked into a river simply because it is nine o'clock on Monday morning, and you are free to do so. Plunging into a roadside water tank, neck-deep, surprisingly cold, and home to a few unexpected goldfish.

Trying to freestyle 'La Marseillaise' on the violin for a drunk man who wanted to sing along. An unpromising busk outside a greengrocer's that astonished me with its generous customers. You play a song; you earn some money; you buy a peach.

Hard days on the hot plains, days I'll remember all my life. All the days of double miles and half-rations when I didn't earn anything. Days when I felt, as Laurie had, 'a deliriously sharpening hunger, an appetite so keen it seemed almost a pity to satisfy it, so voluptuous it was'.

A handful of sweet chestnuts to suck, a gift from a farmer's wife. Bread and carrots for dinner. The decadence of that ice cream. Its crisp chocolate coat and cool satin smoothness!

Counting dwindling coins to the last cent.

A growing confidence. Disbelief at seeing the whole madcap idea work.

And now the end was within reach.

There are many times on a journey when you say, 'I'm walking to X' and people gasp. But there comes the time when the response changes to, 'Oh, that's not far', and the surprise comes instead from telling where you began. A retired dentist was the first to remark on this as I fended off his dog's boisterous leaps in a park. His only surprise about walking to Madrid was how long I still thought it would take: he used to commute daily into the city from here and considered it nearby. The twenty-first-century mind is more adept at imagining trains hurtling beneath mountains than the age-old shuffle of feet over high passes.

This is my favourite stage of an adventure: near enough to the end to grow excited, not so close that you have already begun missing the trip before it's even over. I have learned that this phase always comes when there is about one-tenth of the journey remaining. No matter how long or short the trip, once I'm 90 per cent through I begin to look forward to the finish line, tiring of the drudgery. I can be confident by now that I have what it takes to make it. And once success is possible, there feels little more to prove. My thoughts turn to clean clothes, cold beer and home. Relaxation and company appeal more than masochistic marching.

Cycling round the world, this emotion struck me as I entered Istanbul. Asia lay behind me and I only had Europe to cross, for the second time. The hard miles were over. Walking the Kaveri river in India, the feeling arrived when I crested the forested hills of the Western Ghats in Kerala and knew it was downhill all the way to the ocean. Rowing the Atlantic, our end-of-term mood brewed about four days from landfall, with the twin sensations of desperation to get off the boat and a heightened determination not to capsize and die before then. Not now, not after all this.

Here, as I anticipated Madrid, I was struck by the notion that I had gathered enough of these experiences. More travel stories would be nice, of course. It was the greatest drug of my life. But I already knew the pride of closing in on an objective. I had done it before. I loved it. But this did not mean I needed to keep repeating it. There were other things I needed more than trophy finish lines. Connecting deeply with my family, exploring my own country, rousing a rabble to do the same. Becoming more generous. All this awaited me on the other side of those mountains.

Mountains

BUT FIRST, I HAD to cross the mountains. Silent and still, pure as water. Sounds and movement emerged as I drew closer. Trickling springs, my breath rasping as I gained height to a new world of cowbells, solitary oaks and the smell of crushed thyme underfoot.

I took a shortcut and forded a river. I took off my shoes and socks and waded across. The water was knee-deep, clear and cold, with soft sand and waving weeds underfoot. I had never crossed this stream before. I shall never do so again. There are other rivers, of course, and I'll cross plenty of them in my life. But for now there was just this pleasant moment. If I stared too hard, hoping to sear it upon my retina, the magic of that would disappear.

As I set down my pack to camp for the night, my shirt split right across the shoulders, threadbare from sweat and sun and rucksack rub. A bat flitted past my head in the orange gloaming. I lay on the grassy slopes of a hillside that ran uninterrupted all the way down to the plain. I thought of Laurie Lee and Robert Jordan, who just missed each other up in these mountains. In *For Whom the Bell Tolls*, the fictional Robert Jordan enjoyed a 'walking tour' in the Sierra two years before Laurie's adventure. I was following the footsteps of two of my heroes, and the end of my adventure was within reach. I was in high spirits, despite having only two cents in my pocket. Tramping through Spain had everything I seek in a journey: it was challenging, it was beautiful and it made me happy. Usually, I realised, expeditions provided only the first two. A summer of dusty tracks and a sleeping bag: I did not want or need anything more.

I was on the move again before sunrise, for the night had been cold. The mountains were still dark by the time my limbs had loosened, but the lowlands were already soaked with sunlight and colour. I followed the Roman road, matching my stride to a hundred generations of marching men. Countless soldiers and shepherds, as well as Robert Jordan and Laurie Lee, had climbed this cobbled pass before me, cutting through towards Madrid.

It was such a tranquil morning that I detoured up a side peak just for fun. At the top I found a *refugio*, a simple stone shelter for climbers. The hut boasted a splendid view across the mountains, showing me the lie of the land ahead. The pass used by the Romans was clearly the logical place to head for. The barrier of the mountains dipped to just 1,900 metres there. I wanted to stay in the *refugio*, but breakfast time was a bit early to stop for the day given my limited supplies.

My idea of an idyllic weekend would be to come up into mountains like these for a long run or bike ride with my friends. I was not alone in thinking this. The first couple of hikers took me by surprise, for I had grown used to being alone in Spain, being greeted only by farm workers driving battered Renault vans along bumpy tracks who would call '*¡Venga, hasta luego!*' from their window, then be gone.

I paused as the hikers approached, ready to chat. I was struck by how clean they looked. One even had the audacity to be wearing a white shirt. But to my surprise, they breezed straight past me without speaking. For me, these mountains were the glorious culmination of a 500-mile hike. For them, it was just a footpath near the car park after a short drive with coffee and music. It was good to see the countryside being enjoyed, but when people don't even say *hola* it is too crowded for me.

And so I felt somewhat muted as I crested the ridge. Reaching the Puerto de la Fuenfría meant it was now downhill all the way to Madrid and the end of my journey. This was a literal watershed moment for Laurie, atop the tallest mountain range he had ever seen. 'I rested awhile under towering peaks that were dusted with summer snow . . . Through the pass I saw a new country emerge – the immense plain of La Mancha, stretching flat as a cowhide and smudged like a sore with distant Madrid.'

It should have been a big occasion for me as well, staring south with eagle eyes. But I just shrugged. I was running out of time, so Madrid had to be my finish line. But I mourned the end, rather than celebrating it.

Way Back

I DID NOT WANT to let go of either my walk or these mountains, with their bubbling springs, dappled woods and sunlit ridges above the tree line. I decided to prolong the journey a little and, in the process, reclaim the hills for myself. I studied my map and found a new route, higher and more remote than the logical route southwards.

Stirred by the possibility of a new adventure, I left the day trippers and the trail behind. The terrain was steep and difficult. I concentrated on my breathing and let my mind drift away.

'Can you teach me the violin really quickly?'

'*Está lejos*. It's a long way. Too far to walk.'

Over the next five hours of climbing up and away from the pass, I covered only four miles. My legs burned.

'Even if you don't find happiness you'll at least be living.'

'There are wolves, *lobos*, in the hills.'

It was a fiendish, hands-on-knees ascent, up a narrow and twisting path.

'Bloody hell, I'm going to be forty next year.'

Boulders blocked the way. I clambered up and round and

over them. But I was delighted. I seem to always end my journeys with one last, hard push. I remembered the last hill in Africa, approaching Cape Town, sprinting on my bike with everything I had. For the hard times and for all the good times.

'Give it five, ten, twenty years and then we'll get our own lives back.'

'I can't go on. Please, can we camp now?'

'FUUUUUUUUUUUUUUUUCK!'

The hikers' noisy chatter was far below me now. The forest lay quiet. I was hot, even beneath the shade of the trees. Shafts of sunlight arrowed through the branches. I gulped air and water.

I remembered finishing my walk in India a few months before I became a father. I set out to walk 50 miles on the last day. To see if I could. To show that I could. My future was racing towards me. Was I ready? Here in Spain I was trying to show something to my children. I tightened the waistband on my rucksack, and started upwards again.

'Ben, I'm not coming to Antarctica.'

The ascent turned into a race against myself. As my mind whirred, my legs accelerated. Soon I was climbing flat out. Sweat dripped from my nose. My trousers turned dark with sweat. My breathing was noisy and ragged.

'What adventure are you planning next?'

'"Talk to me," said the doctor.'

Sweat ran down my sunglasses, and I wiped my eyes. The salt stung. I blew my nose on my sleeve and kept climbing. Drool dangled from my mouth as I struggled for air.

'The silences make a tune. The pauses are what make a life. My name is Antonio. Now, play me "Guantanamera" again.'

'Here is my story. Now tell me yours.'

I chuckled at the prospect of bumping into anyone. They would think me mad, charging alone up this mountain trail.

'You could leave. Why don't you?'

'You asked for it. It's up to you now.'

I looked upwards, praying I was near the top. But I could not see through the trees. I didn't know how far I still had to go, only that I was not there yet. I screwed my face into a grimace and sprinted for the summit.

'From this day forward, for better or for worse.'

'¡Soy el rey del mundo!'

'Here comes the sun, little darling.'

Just when I thought I could not keep going, that I had failed and burned myself out, I crested the range at last. It was over. I collapsed in a heap on a smooth rock, gasping, sweating, my head spinning. I slipped my shoulders from the rucksack straps, exhausted, then slumped forwards, chuckling. My legs trembled and drops of sweat fell from my forehead. When my breathing settled, I reached into my bag and pulled out a squashed hunk of bread. I chewed with the languid, satiated feeling that it was all over now.

Now, on the ridge of the Siete Picos, I could raise my arms and whoop at the sky, releasing the emotion of journey's end. I had come a long way through dark places to get here. I set up my camera with the self-timer to capture this memory, and ran to pose for my photograph, facing south towards Madrid. I knew that the worst of times were behind me, that I was entering a fresh chapter of my life. I could see for miles ahead. The view was wonderful. I was facing away when the shutter clicked, so the camera did not capture the smile on my face. But I know it was there.

'Crossing the Sierra was not just a stage on my journey,

in spite of the physical barrier,' wrote Laurie. 'It was also one of those sudden, jerky advances in life, which once made closes the past for ever.'

The few trees that grew at these heights were ancient, twisted and stunted. I clipped my rucksack shut, then lifted it off the ground, shivering as the pack pressed my sodden shirt against my skin. The mad burst of energy had passed. All afternoon I picked my way slowly through purple heather scattered among the rocks. The wind and altitude kept me cool. For the first time in weeks I didn't hide from the afternoon heat. I dropped down to another pass, a ski resort of concrete hotels and ski-lift machinery, ugly and exposed without snow. A tour bus disgorged pale British pensioners to photograph the view among leather-clad bikers on a day ride from Madrid. I didn't want to see British people, didn't want anyone to talk to me in English. Once again, I fled back into the hills.

I sweated up a steep track. Herds of ibex grazed in the soft evening sunshine, clattering across the scree as I approached. This route was a renowned climb in Spain's greatest bike race, the Vuelta a España. Fans had painted cyclists' names and slogans on the road, daubed ghosts of cheering crowds and grimacing riders. Tonight, though, the mountain was all mine.

I was still walking over the rolling plateau at sunset. It would have been sensible to camp down in the relative warmth of the previous pass. But I was giddy with these hills and willing to trade a night of broken sleep for extra time up on the heights.

The first stars appeared, followed by the lights from towns below. One by one at first, but then in a rush until they outshone the stars. It was the beginning of the city which meant the end for me. I wanted to linger up here, living the simple life, moving from spring to spring, alone and at peace. But my stomach was urging me down. I had eaten nothing but white bread for two days. I was hungry and gassy, and on tight rations until I earned some money.

I contoured to the head of a new valley and dropped down from a spring. Its flow was no greater than a trickle, but it would become the river I followed all the way to Madrid. I decided to lose altitude, for the night cold was already creeping in. The valley curved around on three sides like a grassy bowl. I galloped down beside the stream. I found a perfect camp spot, flat and soft with moss, shaded from the wind, alongside a chain of pools and small waterfalls.

I put on every layer of clothing I had. Then I rigged the tarpaulin over my sleeping bag to keep out the cold a little. I shivered, but had to accept and endure it. I turned off my alarm to allow myself a lie-in. But my body woke at the usual time from habit, and I was too cold to indulge in idleness. So I packed up and continued down the valley, warmth seeping into my body as sunlight crept through the hills.

River

FOLLOWING A RIVER IS one of my favourite gateways into a journey. Follow any stream and you become an explorer, discovering places and thoughts entirely new to you. Like me, rivers are on restless missions. The difference between us is that they accept the direction they are flowing and don't wish they were heading anywhere else.

And what a river this was! My tiny stream grew into one of the most beautiful rivers of my life. The Río Manzanares began like a Lake District brook, bouncing through the heather and ferns. I followed it in a state of elation as it moved through labyrinths of granite cliffs, caves and balanced boulders beneath a jagged skyline. Laurie was equally enchanted, 'gulping the fine, dry air and sniffing the pitch-pine mountain, I was perhaps never so alive and so alone again'. As the valley closed in, tight and forested now, the river grew as it dropped between deep, smooth pools scooped out by waterfalls.

Along a typical river, any of these would have been ideal

for a swim. But on this special day I could be picky, pushing
on from pool to pool to find the best. Each was a little larger,
a little deeper, a little more perfect than the last. The sun
stirred the forest's scent, a perfume of hot dust and pine
needles. The temperature rose and soon it was time to take
the plunge.

I waded first into a shaded cleft of river, narrow and deep,
with trout zipping up and down. The water was 'snow-cold,
brutal, and revivifying'. I gasped as I entered, belly tensed
and arms held high. I whimpered as the water reached my
crotch. I plunged under the water then towelled myself dry
with my shirt, shivering and goose-pimpled. But it was invig-
orating. You never regret a swim once you're out and warm
again.

I learned later that swimming in the Río Manzanares had
been banned. Its proximity to Madrid means that people have
caused too much damage to this important Natural Reserve.
I didn't know this, so I swam several times. In my defence,
I left no trace behind once the echoes of my squeals had
faded.

My second dip was in a sunny hollow – hot face and cold
toes – with rapids bubbling the water and the view funnelled
back up the valley towards the river head where I camped the
night before. The third swim – the crowning glory – was in
a pool which must have been popular before the ban. Amorous
couples had carved initials and hearts into the rock. It was
known as *El Pozo Verde*, 'the green puddle'. Boulders big as
buses made the scramble down to it tricky, but it was worth
the effort. *El Pozo Verde* was the biggest pool along the river,
about 15 metres across. The water was deep and clear and
motionless. Beside the pool was a slick, silvery slab of rock,

hot to the touch and smooth. It made a perfect slide. I hurtled down the rock into the water. It was the most enjoyable five seconds of my summer. Plunging deep into the pool was like slipping inside an emerald.

Thunder Road

BACK BEFORE I EVER picked up a violin, there was one song I always imagined playing on this walk. I pictured crowds hurling money at my feet. Women wanting to be with me. Men wanting to be me. This was all until the reality of my musical incompetence hit home!

Even once I ditched the delusion of cheers and tears, I persevered with learning 'Thunder Road', albeit only managing a rudimentary grasp of the opening and closing bars. I have listened to its eulogising of hope and hitting the road count-less times, loud and quiet, happy and sad, taking off for places new, on late-night drives to the mountains, or gnashing with caged bitterness under the sodium glow of suburban skies. The song's cry to redemption and leaving the past behind fitted this journey and the reasons I was here. Even if I could only play eight bars, I wanted to at least bring its spirit to Spain.

The song opens with those long harmonica notes breaking your heart (before the screen door slams and Mary's dress waves). They worked well on the violin, and I practised them hard, singing for the lonely, and the fear of not being able to face myself alone again. The drug I kept seeking in Spain, scared but craving it, was vulnerability: standing in plazas time after time and asking the question, will you hear me play? How will you respond? How will I respond?

The dread of time passing in 'Thunder Road' strikes me harder every year. It's what I see in the mirror, 40 looming, a gnawing worry in my mind. But there is hope, too, if I can show some faith. There's magic in these white-hot Spanish streets. I'm not good at what I am doing. My life is not where I had imagined it would be. I have been frustrated with myself, disappointed, tempted to give up. It's no beauty. But, honestly, I know it's all right. It's more than that. The distance this escapade put between me and my real life was showing me that perspective.

I was not wasting my summer praying in vain for some saviour to rise and fix it all for me. I was out here trying to do it myself. I was no hero for this; I understood that. All the redemption I was looking for came just from this violin and my dirty hiking shoes. I was determined to turn myself around. To go home a better man. Otherwise what else would I do except keep hitting the road forever?

The open road leads anywhere, that is addictively true. And the triumphant exultation of letting the wind blow back your hair as you barrel towards unknown adventures is what I have tried to bottle for years. But was it only luring me on because of the flawed hope that when I reached 'there' – wherever there might be – everything would be better than 'here'? The folly was obvious. Wherever I go, my baggage will be there, and the promised land once again gone on the wind to the rainbow's end.

I was trying to stop running away and choosing instead to head somewhere worth walking towards. I was learning to grapple with an adult life full of compromise. I saw my situation with more gratitude now: I had a home, rewarding work, enough money, and the two best kids in the world. From faraway Spain, I could look at my ordinary life with the sense of wonder I used to reserve for waking on a mountaintop in a distant land.

Back when I was cycling round the world, I sent Sarah a Valentine's rose from Tokyo. I was living on two dollars a day so the gesture was extravagant. We were not a couple then, but I had been thinking of Sarah and dreaming of a life with her: travelling the world together, sharing the adventure.

On the card sent with the rose, I quoted 'Thunder Road', asking whether Sarah was willing to take the hardest step of all, from her doorstep out into the unknown. It was a long walk to Bruce's car and his new life together with Mary, a long way between wanting to fix my life, talking about it and actually making it happen. But I was on my way.

Last Play

I FOLLOWED THE BEAUTIFUL river until the land opened up and the valley released me. I was exhausted. Walking downhill hurt. Walking uphill hurt. Walking on the flat hurt. My shortage of food had taken its toll. My legs trembled and my vision was blurred. I trudged towards a town, Manzanares el Real, dreaming of food, but needing money to buy it. On the outskirts, overlooking the river and mountains, were the most exclusive homes I passed in all of Spain. Built from stone, with ornate gates and high hedges, they flaunted their wealth. A red Mercedes turned into a drive and I glimpsed green lawns and flowerbeds before the electric gate slid shut.

I hurried onwards, limping on sore feet. Vultures circled on thermals, scanning for opportunities. Everything irritated me as I made my way towards the town centre. Mopeds buzzed and traffic lights held me up. I reached the plaza at last. It was lively with families and hung with bunting, alternating strands of little Spanish flags and EU stars. Old folk sat on benches on the perimeter and kids skidded their bikes or hoofed footballs. There was a cheerful murmur to the evening. This was the final place I would busk before Madrid. I was here to earn money, but I also wanted to enjoy it and remember it.

I began the familiar routine of setting up to play. Take out the violin and set the open case on the ground, just in case. Unfold the music stand. Peg down the sheets. I felt this final performance ought to be meaningful, to reveal some sort of lesson. But I was too hungry to think very deeply. I looked around the plaza, weighing up my chances, and rubbed the bow with rosin to give it grip. You need friction to play beautiful notes.

I didn't know yet if this musical escapade would prove significant in my life. I tested the tuning, first the A string, then the E, as Becks had taught me. Perhaps I would go home better able to embrace what I had, with all its joys and irritations. I felt more comfortable with myself out here, willing to be kinder to myself, and therefore more able to be kind to others.

I shuffled the sheets of paper until I found the song I always started with. God, it was a relief to let go of what I *thought* I should be. To just accept who I actually was, vulnerabilities and all. I played a couple of tentative notes to break the meniscus of silence. A few heads turned. Maybe trying to earn my next meal was enough, learning to live simply. This adventure would take time to sink in. That was fine by me. I had plenty of time. I began to play.

> *Yo soy un hombre sincero*
> *De donde crece la palma.*
> *Y antes de morir yo quiero*
> *Echar mis versos del alma.*

I am an honest man,
From the place where the palm tree grows.
And before I die I want to
Sing out the verses of my soul.

Two teenagers stopped to listen – a chatty, chubby girl on rollerblades and a serious boy in thick spectacles. They were intrigued by the novelty of a dirty foreign hiker coming all the way to their little town to play his violin badly. They each gave me 50 cents.

But that was all for an hour or more. I played and played, but nobody cared. A couple watching me from the terrace of a bar got the joke and laughed over their glasses of wine. Everyone else just carried on enjoying the summer evening as they had been doing before I'd turned up. Some parents regarded me as easy childcare, for I attracted an audience of children. I was amused by them at first, but they became noisy as their numbers increased, hampering my chances of earning anything.

Fortunately, three old ladies chattering on a bench behind me saved the evening. They called me over and gave me a few coins. They all clucked and tutted and fussed and spoke at the same time.

'You need a *refresco*, a drink of pop,' said one.

'You look tired,' worried the second.

'You need to sit and rest,' added the third.

'I certainly do, *señoras*,' I agreed. 'But first, I really, really have to eat something. Thank you so much for helping me.'

And I made a beeline for the supermarket.

I spent 10 minutes slumped on the floor inside the supermarket entrance, absorbing the coldness of the marble and the soothing darkness of indoors. I was sun-fried, and it took time for my body and brain to settle sufficiently so that I was able to calculate what I could afford. To my surprise, I shied away from spending all my money as I had been accustomed to doing ever since Vigo. I saved some for Madrid. I knew it was cowardly. But I always get nervous in cities and did not want to add being penniless to my worries.

I camped on a stretch of roadside grass just out of town, beyond the lights, by a lake that turned bronze in the twilight. A cow waded in the shallows, rippling the smooth water, and I lay on top of my sleeping bag and ate a banana. Then I fell asleep looking up at the skyline of the mountains I had crossed, sandwiched between the street lights and the North Star.

The Wall

THE TOWNS EXPANDED NOW, satellite settlements for the capital merging into one another. I walked a few miles with Pablo, a retired 63-year-old out for his morning walk. When our paths crossed he was walking briskly with his headphones on and shirt off. He was tanned and lean and I had to speed up to match his stride. Pablo had worked in the IT department at Iberia airline for 40 years. He had hated the job, but it paid well and *'trabajo es trabajo*, work is work'. Now Pablo had moved to the outskirts of Madrid to 'start enjoying life'. He had lost various lengths of intestine to cancer and was delighted now by retirement and his chance to savour life. I was horrified at the prospect of waiting for retirement and rehab to begin enjoying life, but also inspired by how sprightly he was.

Waving goodbye to Pablo, I got lost behind a factory and opted for a shortcut down a scrubby slope. Sliding down, scratched and cursing, my shoes filled with spiky grass seeds. A man watched, perplexed, from the bottom. He waited until

I emerged from the undergrowth to warn me, somewhat late, about the risk of vipers, with their triangular heads, zigzag stripes and toxic bite.

I continued through an industrial estate and made my way back out onto *dehesa*, open farmland dotted with oak trees. There, in front of me, a viper basked on the footpath. It was the colour of summer dust, with a stark, dark zigzag, and orange eyes. I admired the sinuous movement as it smoothly retreated from me. I admired my calmness for not panicking. Then, rounding the next corner, I saw a curved stick lying on the path and jumped out of my skin.

The day was baking hot, one of the fiercest of them all. Spain was not letting me go without a fight. There was a lake in the distance, an ideal siesta spot if I could find some shade. I put my head down and limped onwards. To my dismay, a high wall barricaded the lake. It was unlike anything I had seen in Spain, where homes are walled in but the countryside rarely so. But I was too hot to give it much thought. A silly wall would not keep me from a swim. I chucked over my pack, climbed up, jumped down and dived in. The lake was tranquil, or at least it had been until my arrival scattered storks, deer, a wild boar and her piglet.

After the swim, I endured the worst siesta of the summer. I could only find partial shade beneath scraggy carob trees, so I sweated for hours wearing all my clothes and my hat to protect me from sunburn. I was extremely uncomfortable. Studying my map and planning the route into Madrid, I realised that the wall I had jumped over was marked on the map and stretched for many miles. It appeared to surround a royal palace! I could not be certain of that, but what was indisputable was that it created a significant detour. I was not in the mood for detours, not even for royalty. A combination of the violent heat and end-of-journey apathy led to me hatching the genius plan of just ignoring the wall and hoping to feign innocence if anyone caught me.

So I continued walking inside the wall, heading south towards the city. I followed a wide road, smooth and well maintained. There was no traffic, so I walked straight down the middle. Eagles soared and circled above hoopoes and parakeets. There was wildlife everywhere. On I went through the strange silence. Scores of deer grazed in the long grass, both stags and fawns. Whenever they caught my scent, they ran, flowing across the land into the safety of trees. They fled with the shock of creatures unaccustomed to seeing humans. Where on earth was I? The world had receded. What was this weird place? *Was* it a royal palace? Suddenly, lions roared into my imagination. What if this was a safari park?! I was going crazy. I needed water. I rested in the lee of an elm tree for a few minutes, summoning the energy for one more push to water. When the road reached the stagnant lake once again, I submerged my head and drank.

Towards sunset, I spotted another wall. The road led up to electric gates topped with barbed wire. I approached the wall, intrigued but nervous. All was about to be revealed. Where was I? Would I get arrested? Hopefully, they would at least give me a drink first.

The security guard in the little checkpoint booth was facing, correctly, outwards. I tapped on the window to catch his attention. This made him jump. He swivelled his chair angrily. Not a good start. Never annoy a bored minor official and give them the rare opportunity to test their powers. The guard's belly bulged beneath the untucked shirt of a crumpled green uniform. He hauled himself to his feet and reached for a button to open the gate.

We both waited for the gate to slide open, looking at each other and wondering what was going to happen next. I walked through to meet the guard and my fate. He looked me up and down – a dirty foreigner with a rucksack and a violin – and asked what the hell I was doing.

I bluffed cheerfully, pretending not to understand a word of Spanish. I smiled at him as though I was delighted to bump into an old friend. Lovely to meet you! Mimed how hot it was. *¡Scorchio!* Blooming thirsty! No idea I had done anything untoward. Pointed down the road. Made some walking motions with my fingers. Queried, 'Madrid?' Be super if you could confirm I am heading the right way, pal. Then I'll be on my way. Really appreciate it. Nice to chat, but I'd better get on . . .

But the guard raised his hands to silence me and made it clear I could not leave. My idiot charades had flummoxed him. He returned to his booth and phoned the boss. I watched him glancing at me through the window as he described me. The guard hung up the phone and reappeared with his notebook. It had Bugs Bunny on the cover: this was official now. I gave my name, address and phone number. All fake. I sensed that I wasn't going to get into much trouble. The tension had gone. As the guard's humour improved, so did my Spanish. Soon we were talking happily.

The area I had walked through had once been a royal hunting ground, and was now a pristine ecological reserve, a special protection area. I felt guilty about this: I would far rather disturb royalty than rare animals. Entry to the sanctuary was strictly forbidden. The guard rolled his eyes at my idiocy. But he let me go at last, and we shook hands. I was pleased to escape and relieved not to have been sent back to walk the long way round. For I was weary now, heavy with the tiredness which comes once you know that the end of a journey has begun.

Last Night

I REJOINED MY RIVER, though in my absence it had grown slow and suburban. I camped beside it in a park on the fringes of Madrid. I tucked out of sight of the evening dog walkers and joggers among a grove of willow trees. It was the first night I had taken care to conceal myself, sensing now the presence of a big city. Mosquitoes whined, and trains and sirens disturbed the night.

I wriggled into my sleeping bag and bundled together a pillow from my jacket and shoes. Then I checked my map by the light of my head torch, calculating and recalculating how long it would take me to get into Madrid. I was so close now. Sleep eluded me beneath the sodium orange sky as I imagined being reunited with my family. I was eager to put the new me to the test, the unfurling chrysalis I had sensed in Spain. I pictured hugging Tom and Lucy, and smiling at Sarah over their heads. I had described them earlier in my diary as 'without doubt my two favourite people in the whole world'. For all that my children wore me down, they gave back so much more.

Becoming a parent had been a stern test. It challenged me

to stop racing and to consider what kind of a person I would become. My kids knew nothing about my consternation and struggles. They didn't care. They were just happy to jump on their dad, beaming with unconditional love every time I came home. I was confident now that by the time they were old enough to be perceptive to such things, Tom and Lucy could love and respect the man they saw dancing badly in the kitchen. The pram in the hall was no longer my enemy. It would be my inspiration, giving me the resolve to write better books and live adventurously within the framework of our family life. Things felt more balanced now, the smiles returning to all our faces. For too long I had thought adventure was life. But, actually, life is the adventure. And that is not the same thing at all. Oh, Sarah, how I looked forward to the years ahead.

> Little darling, I feel that ice is slowly melting
> Little darling, it seems like years since it's been clear
> Here comes the sun . . .

Busking in Spain had only been a modest adventure. It would not win the grudging praise I used to crave from hard men in gaffer-patched down jackets sipping pints of bitter. But in its own way this had been one of the most adventurous challenges of my life, right up there with cycling the world or walking around the M25 – arguably the two most interesting journeys I have taken. I had found it consistently quite hard, and 'quite hard', at last, sounded enough for me.

My ambition in recent years has been to become *less* ambitious, trying to trade my restless drive for a calmer contentment more compatible with life as a husband and a father. In exchange, I could accept both a journey and a life which is only 'quite hard'. I was trying to concede that I had probably wandered enough. Continuing with more of the same was the easy option. More of a challenge was admitting that, while it had been glorious, it was time for something different. I was making progress at what poet Mary Oliver described as allowing 'the voodoos of ambition' to sleep. Trading them for stillness, instead.

My path is no longer guided by big expeditions. Those days are gone. I won't see the whole world. But I've stopped chasing that to try to build a simple, kind and happy life with my family. I'm sure this was the correct decision, that it outshines any of my own adventures. Rather than torturing myself with all the different permutations of how life might have run, it makes more sense to slam the menu shut and try to relish the life I chose. I cherish running in the small mountains of the Lake District, for example, driving north by myself once my family are in bed, frost in the headlights, stars bright above the silhouettes of those familiar peaks. I could run for the rest of my days in those hills without knowing them all. The grail I am searching for – a worthwhile life – is available everywhere. I will not trek to the South Pole. But there are other South Poles in the lives of men.

We all dream of achieving the extraordinary in our lives, our personal version of trekking to the South Pole. Having failed myself, but eventually come out the other end smiling, I now believe there is something even more important than striving for the remarkable. And that is to stop dreaming about an 'adventure of a lifetime', and instead pursue a lifetime of living adventurously through a daily pledge to push myself a little, scare myself now and then, and remain curious.

I have thrown off my old attitudes about adventure being rugged men doing rugged stuff in rugged places. It is much broader than that. Living adventurously is an attitude with which you charge at life, and it applies whether you cycle across a continent, climb a nearby hill, or take up a musical instrument. It demands only that you stretch yourself, even if that just involves playing a violin in front of a handful of people in a sunny plaza.

I know I can't cure my wanderlust. I'm not sure I would want to. But at least I now have a better understanding of why travel was such a big part of me for so long. Alongside wanting to explore the world was an insecure drive to prove something, both to myself and as a snarled 'fuck you' to everything that made me feel mediocre when I was young. It was explosive fuel when mixed with wanderlust and a determination to live a full life, both exhilarated and anxious about what the future might hold.

I cannot justify yearning for adventure. That longing never leaves you. Travel has given me some of the richest experiences of my life. For a long time, it meant everything to me. Bruce Springsteen sang the soundtrack to many of those years, so his words are fitting as my life changes tack. 'When you walk onstage tonight to bring the noise, treat it like it's all we have – and then remember it's only rock 'n' roll.'

Into Madrid

WALKING INTO CITIES IS always tedious, so I was delighted to find a perfect route into Madrid, a swathe of green space arrowing deep into the city. But my plan was foiled. It turned out to be more bloody palace grounds, though guarded this time by grumpy men with guns. They shooed me away and I rejoined the crowds and commoners.

I set to the struggle of entering, on foot, a world designed for cars. I picked my way through the morning madness, shaking my fist at speeding drivers, yelling at a bus that swerved to a stop in front of me. The pace of city life shocked me. After weeks living at walking speed, cars looked fast and dangerous as they hammered towards me, straight into the glare of the sun. A blinking indicator or an early fade of direction reassured me that they had spotted me. But the late-swervers, the no-swervers and the phone-texters frightened me.

I got lost and went around in circles. My heart thumped as I tried to hurry. But cars hooted their anger, and my head ached with fumes and the rumble of traffic. I sat on a pavement and drank some water. My clothes were filthy. I smelled awful. I sensed passers-by averting their eyes or darting looks of disapproval. I stared through a forest of walking legs. I was no longer a busker. I was a bum. A vagrant, not a visitor. Not a troubadour but a tramp. The notion that had kept me going, of being on a noble little quest, dissolved on that street.

I hate navigating big cities. I had gritted my teeth through this many times. I thought about my years of cycling stubbornly into vast cities, the hours of terror and tedium negotiating the madness of Tokyo, Mexico City, Los Angeles or Cairo. But today, all of a sudden, I couldn't be bothered any more. I had had enough.

Laurie had also known the impatience of nearing a long-anticipated city – in his case London – of being both attracted and repelled by all that awaited. 'I hurried towards [the city], impatient now, its sulphur stinging my nostrils. I had been a month on the road, and the suburbs were long and empty. In the end, I took a tube.'

For the final time, I asked myself, 'What would Laurie do?'

I counted the last of my coins and smiled. Then I descended into the nearest Metro station, and settled in a comfortable, air-conditioned carriage. Shortly afterwards, I emerged blinking in the heart of Madrid.

August in the capital. The streets saturated with heat. *Madrileños* flee for the coast or recline in the darkness of their homes, windows shuttered against the glare. I entered a small deserted bar on the Calle Echegaray.

'*Buenos días*. How much does a large, cold beer cost?'

'*Dos cincuenta.*'

'Thank you. I'll be back.'

I found a park, noisy with birdsong and buses. It was busy, but nobody spoke or acknowledged anyone else. Office workers brushed past at speed, shiny shoes and suits, phones and cigarettes. Stooped old ladies shuffled along with their shopping bags. Nannies ambled with prams. A muttering homeless man scouted for cigarette ends.

'Welcome back to the world, Humphreys,' I thought as I unzipped my case and lifted out the violin one last time.

The embarrassment and doubt of my first day's busking flooded back. City busking requires more than just turning up. It demands talent and a thick skin. I had neither. But I had done this many times now. What you practise is who you become. Playing the violin had meant acknowledging my weaknesses so that I could begin to make strengths of them instead. If you want to get somewhere, you must take a step in the right direction. Perhaps once this is all over, I thought, I should write about my struggles. The openness might help someone. It would certainly have helped me to read something similar a few years ago.

Craftsmen in Japan mix gold dust into the lacquer when repairing shattered pottery. They call it *kintsugi*. Rather than disguising the damage with invisible glue, as we do, *kintsugi* embraces the imperfections and repairs as part of the object's history. It becomes unique and beautiful. Like fragile ceramic, we too face a life of cracks and knocks, especially if we risk living adventurously. But, with time and care, our broken selves can be put back together. Forget your perfect offering, there is a crack in everything. We should feel no shame in wearing our golden scars with pride.

From Atlantic-sized terror a month ago to a small shrug today: I rolled up my sleeves and got on with it. I wanted a beer. It was time for *The Muppet Show* theme tune. How apt. I scraped my way to beer money, then returned to the bar.

Home from Abroad

LAURIE CONTINUED SOUTH FROM Madrid until he reached the Mediterranean. He cherished the memories of his walk for the rest of his life. His time in Spain, Laurie realised, had been 'perhaps the easiest, loneliest, and best time of my life'. At the onset of the civil war, the Royal Navy evacuated him from Almuñécar.

In the winter of 1937, Laurie slipped over the Pyrenees and back into Spain, to join the ranks of the International Brigades in the fight against fascism. But they found him to be 'physically weak, he will not be of any use at the front', though he seemed 'a perfectly sincere comrade'. Laurie remained with the Brigades for just nine weeks. Ever after, he obfuscated about the experience, in part from shame about his peripheral involvement in the war. Only in 1991 did Laurie publish his stories about that winter in what was to be his final book, *A Moment of War*.

After Spain, Laurie settled in London, writing film scripts and occasional books and poems. He was gregarious but reserved, once confessing, 'all I want from life is ten pounds a week and no questions asked'. He married and became a father. Like me, Laurie found it both a bind and the richest joy of his life. In the 1960s he returned to live in Slad, his childhood village in the Cotswolds. Despite many travels and adventures, he 'never found a place which has such intimate significance' as the area in which he grew up.

So do I breathe the hayblown airs of home,
And watch the sea-green elms drip birds and shadows,
And as the twilight nets the plunging sun
My heart's keel slides to rest among the meadows.

Laurie Lee died in 1997, aged 82, with his wife and daughter by his bedside. He requested to be buried, so the story goes, halfway between the pub and the church so that he could enjoy the singing on Saturday night and again on Sunday morning. Laurie's gravestone at Holy Trinity Church, only yards from where he was born, reads, 'He lies in the valley he loved'.

Reward

I ORDERED A COLD beer at the bar, then settled outside
at a shaded table. I took off my shoes and socks and rested
my bare feet on my rucksack. My trouser hems had frayed
and my red shirt faded. I pushed my sunglasses up onto my
head, wiped my face and ate the last of my bread.

The *camarero* brought my beer and presented the change
on a silver dish. I gave it back to him as a tip. The waiter
may not have appreciated it much – just a few small coins –
but it was all the money I had, and my own gesture of
kindness to a stranger. It was a small *gracias* to this land of
strangers who had treated me like a guest.

Part of me wished that my journey could continue. My
summer with Laurie Lee had been so enjoyable. But now that
I knew I could busk my way across a country – or a continent
– I did not need to continue. I had wondered for years whether
it was possible. Now I had the answer. 'Spain drifted away
from me, thunder-bright on the horizon, and I left it there
beneath its copper clouds.' I rested my hand on my violin case.
As Laurie wrote in 'April Rise', perhaps his most celebrated

poem – the words engraved on the back of his gravestone – 'If ever I saw blessing in the air I see it now in this still early day'. This was enough. Maybe I was finally learning.

I looked at my beer and held back from taking the first sip. I had anticipated this for so long. I could wait a little longer. I sighed. Sat back. Lifted the glass to the sun. Shining gold, like all those coins. I thought back to those dusty white roads through the orange groves. Summer heat and the tang of citrus. Cicadas shrilling in the still silence. The blue smudge of distant mountains. The days long and open and free. Nowhere to be but here. The roads I took and the choices I made along the way.

I looked out at the street. Down at my dusty feet. Back at all the years of adventure. Forward to whatever might unfold next. You will have your reward. And I thought to myself, yes, the life that I could still live, I should live.

'Cheers,' I smiled to myself, and raised the frosted glass to my lips.

It's All Right

It is Sunday and I am cooking lunch at home. Our friends are late, so I sit at the kitchen table for a few minutes of peace. I no longer feel that desperate clutching at time as I had in my mad days of chucking bicycles into fields. This morning I woke, as usual, at half-five to go to the gym and blast away some excess energy. As I rested between exercises, I received a message from my friend Ben.

'Hello from the South Pole!'

I grabbed my phone. Antarctica rushed back into my life. This was the second time Ben had made it to the bottom of the world since I had pulled out of our expedition. After bashing out some press-ups, I sat down to reply.

'Well done, Ben! Fantastic trip. I really enjoyed following it. I hope you're looking forward now to getting married, bike riding, and maybe writing a book at last? Sounds like a good year to me . . .

Happy New Year, and well done!
Al'

I will always be wistful about Antarctica and a life of big adventure. But a hill run or a lake swim satisfies me these days, more or less. I did a few more press-ups, then headed home to make my kids pancakes for breakfast.

And now, with lamb roasting in the oven and music playing, I sneak an early glass of wine. Tom and Lucy are laughing together on the carpet next door, their heads bowed over a pile of Lego. Sarah lies on the sofa in her jeans, bare feet resting on a cushion, reading the Sunday papers.

Here I am at home, in the domestic box I raged against for years. But I am no longer rattling the cage. Spain did not fix me. I still struggle with being too restless for ordinary life. I would much prefer to live in the mountains than suburbia. But the mindset my journey through Spain demanded, the values it made me aware of – my problems to own, my good times to enjoy – had brought home the way I ought to behave.

I'm older now, drinking wine, and the sweet smells of cooking come drifting through. I skip through the songs to 'Here Comes the Sun'. I begin to cry. My kids will laugh at me if they catch me. This is a whole book of tears. But at least it ends with tears of gratitude and love after too much frustration and sadness. I grab a felt-tip pen from the kids' homework pile to scribble these thoughts, for this feels like the way I want to end my story.

Leave me here, at home, with my family, and winter sunlight streaming through the windowpanes. I travelled to the fields of Spain to look for treasure. I laugh because now I finally know where my treasure is.

My only concern is that our friends arrive before my master-piece roast potatoes spoil (parboil 'em, shake 'em fluffy, cook 'em hot). The house is filled with music, sunshine and laughter.

> Here comes the sun
> Here comes the sun, and I say
> It's all right . . .

As if on cue, an argument breaks out next door. I hear Lego being hurled! I'm needed. But not here, not with you. There's no adventure in this, no story for you any longer. But there is, I see now, a life. My life. Our life.

Acknowledgements

THANK YOU, FIRST OF all, to Laurie Lee for sending me on this adventure, and for setting a high bar for travel writers. (I would encourage everyone to read *As I Walked Out One Midsummer Morning*.)

Thank you also to:

Sally for your optimism and good humour which made all this possible. Karen for much-needed supplementary help.

The kind strangers who supported me in Spain.

Sergio and Sagrario for inviting a wandering, weary Englishman into your home, just when I needed it. Ben and Franchi for welcoming me, smelly and hungry, into your tiny, pregnant, happy apartment in Madrid.

Jessica Woollard, Kate, Rob, Andy, Jo, Franny, Sarah and Anthony for reading drafts and offering useful direction. Numerous other people offered comment or criticism on segments of the book. Rob in particular was pleasingly brutal, showing me that I needed to tell less! Julith Jedamus made many improvements. Javier polished *mi Español*.

Julia Koppitz and Myles Archibald: you are always insightful but relaxed to work with. Hazel Eriksson toiled extremely hard on the edit. Valerie Grove's well-researched biography of Laurie Lee was invaluable, and all the quotes that are not from *As I Walked Out One Midsummer Morning* come from her book.

And, as always, thank you to Sarah, for letting me go, holding the fort, welcoming me home, and generally putting up with me.

The Violin Case

BUSKING BETWEEN VIGO AND Madrid over the course of a month, I earned far more than I had ever dared to hope for. I lived like a king! €125.40 (plus cheap flights) was the total cost of an adventure I will cherish forever.

From the minute I earned my first coin, the entire experience was uplifting, rewarding and wonderful. That is certainly to the detriment of this book, which would have benefited from some disasters! The reality was that the trip proved to be much easier, more fun and less hungry than I had anticipated it would be. This has been true with almost every adventure I have been on, a reminder not to let pessimistic fears stop us attempting things which may turn out to be magical.

I am very glad I sent that spontaneous email from the train.

After the trip I donated €125.40 to Hope and Homes for Children, for I was aware that I had only played at being poor in Spain. There are far too many people in the world who need the kindness of those who donated to me more than I ever will.

If you have enjoyed this book, perhaps you could also flick a virtual coin or two into the charity violin case here: www. hopeandhomes.org/donate.

On a personal level, I would be extremely grateful if you could take a minute to review this book online, on Amazon or whichever website you choose. It makes an enormous difference for authors.

Thank you.

About the Author

Alastair Humphreys' musical career peaked with passing Grade 1 violin after returning from Spain, and earning three dollars in tips when playing to an audience of a thousand in Las Vegas (during one of his talks). He then retired from music while at the peak of his powers.

Alastair is an Adventurer and Keynote Speaker from Yorkshire. He has written books about walking across India and cycling round the world, both for adults and children. His popular *Microadventures* book encourages people to include short, simple, local adventures in their busy lives, while *Grand Adventures* focuses on making adventure accessible to all. It tackles the biggest hurdles many of us face in life: summoning the nerve to begin something new, bold and exciting in our lives.

Alastair was named as one of *National Geographic's* Adventurers of the Year for 2012, but is more proud of the shed where he writes (or, on hot days, up in the treehouse he nominally built for his children). He lives in suburbia, dreams of the mountains and loves jumping into rivers with his family.

Follow Alastair's future adventures:

Monthly newsletter: www.alastairhumphreys.com
YouTube adventure videos, including films from Spain: Search
'Alastair Humphreys' on YouTube.
Instagram and Twitter: @al_humphreys